8541

DATE DUE		
JAN 2 6 2004		
MAY 1 7 2004		

974.4
FRA

Fradin, Dennis B.

The Massachusetts
colony

8541

716090 02250   02372C   001

The
Massachusetts Colony

by Dennis B. Fradin

Consultant: Lynn Parisi
Social Science Education Consortium, Inc.

 CHILDRENS PRESS ®
CHICAGO

Acknowledgment

For their help, the author thanks:

Martha Clark, Reference Supervisor, Massachusetts
State Archives

American Antiquarian Society of Worcester,
Massachusetts

Anthony Fradin

Dedication

For Myron Fradin, with love

Library of Congress Cataloging in Publication Data

Fradin, Dennis B.
The Massachusetts colony.

Includes index.
Summary: A history of the colony, which began with the settling of the
Pilgrims in Plymouth, until its becoming the sixth state of the Union. Includes
brief biographies of notable colonial-era people
1. Massachusetts—History—Colonial period, ca. 1600-1775—
Juvenile literature. 2. Massachusetts—History—Revolution, 1775-1783—
Juvenile literature.
[1. Massachusetts—History—Colonial period, ca. 1600-1775.
2. Massachusetts—History—Revolution, 1775-1783] I. Title.
F67.F78   1986   974.4'02   86-9753
ISBN 0-516-00386-0

10 R 96

Table of Contents

Samoset visits Plymouth Colony

Chapter I

Indians and Early Explorers

Such is [the Indians'] love to one another, that they cannot endure to see their Country-men wronged, but will stand stiffly in their defense. . . . If it were possible to recount the courtesies they have shown the English since their first arrival in those parts, it would not only [convince the Europeans] that they are a loving people, but also win the love of those that never saw them. . . .

William Wood, writing about the Indians in New England's Prospect (1634)

In March of 1621 the Pilgrims who had recently settled in Plymouth, Massachusetts were discussing ways to protect themselves from possible Indian attack. Suddenly a tall, nearly naked Indian walked into their village. The Indian greeted the men by saying, "Welcome, Englishmen!" in their own language. He then told them that his name was Samoset, and that he was a sagamore (chief) of the Pemaquid tribe.

Thus began several decades of friendship between the Indians and the Pilgrims. Because they played so important a role in the colony's early days—and also because they were the people who lived there first—it is with the Indians that the story of the Massachusetts Colony begins.

Before Europeans arrived, many Indian tribes lived in what is now the state of Massachusetts. The Pennacook, Massachusett, Nipmuc, Nauset, Wampanoag, and Pocomtuc were six of the main tribes. Each tribe had its own region. For example, the Massachusett Indians lived in the Boston region and the Wampanoags in southeastern Massachusetts (not including Cape Cod). The Nausets lived on Cape Cod and nearby islands. Some Indians made their homes in what are now several states. For example, the Pennacooks lived in northern Massachusetts and parts of New Hampshire and Vermont.

Indian tribes in Massachusetts

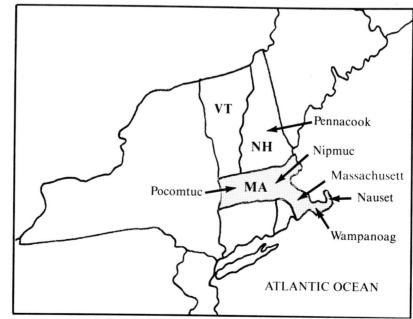

All of the tribes in Massachusetts belonged to the Algonquian family, which occupied much of what is now the eastern United States and Canada. The various Algonquian tribes in Massachusetts had much in common. They spoke dialects of the same language, lived in villages in river valleys or near the ocean, and had similar life-styles.

A typical village was home to about 250 people. It had two kinds of dwellings. Wigwams were dome-shaped cabins made of poles with strips of tree bark laid over them. Inside each wigwam lived a family composed of parents, children, and

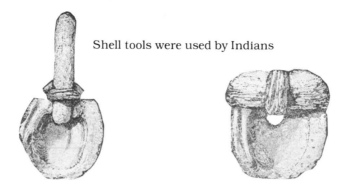

Shell tools were used by Indians

perhaps several other relatives. A longhouse was made of the same materials as a wigwam, but it was larger and oblong in shape. A longhouse was usually home to several related families, each of which had its own section.

The Indians of Massachusetts were able to build permanent villages because they farmed, which meant that they did not have to move from place to place in search of food. The women were the farmers. They tilled the soil with stone hoes, buried fish for fertilizer, then planted seeds. Among their crops were corn, beans, and pumpkins.

The men did the fishing and hunting. They went out in canoes and caught pike, perch, and bass with spears. For larger fish they sometimes used nets. One early English visitor to Massachusetts claimed that the Indians caught eighteen-foot sturgeon in their nets! For hunting, the men used bows and arrows. Indian hunters

Romantic painting of an Indian hunting with a bow and arrow

trained dogs to help them run down moose and deer.

The women cooked the vegetables they had grown and the meat that the men brought home. Little of the slain animals was wasted. The skins were made into clothes and moccasins, bones became needles, turtle shells were used as bowls, and moose sinews made good bowstrings. Unused remains of dead animals were sometimes returned to the streams and fields, so the animals' souls could rest peacefully.

Painting entitled *Death of the Indian Chief Alexander* shows a medicine man praying.

The Indians had no formal schools. Their children learned by observing and listening to their elders. The women taught the girls how to farm, cook, and make clothes. The men taught the boys how to fish, hunt, and make canoes. Both sexes learned their people's history and religious beliefs from the elders.

The Indians worshiped many gods, including gods of the sun, the stars, and other aspects of nature. Indian children were taught to pray to the god of the stream before crossing it, and to leave a gift for the forest god after cutting down a tree. They also heard stories about how the gods had provided such a bountiful world for humankind.

One story told to Wampanoag children explained the origin of corn. According to this story, an old man named Mondomin was so hungry that he prayed to the Great Spirit for food. The next moment Mondomin heard fluttering above his wigwam and found a partridge tangled in the roof. Mondomin roasted the partridge, but before he could take the first bite he heard crying. Back outside, Mondomin found a starving woman. The old man gave his roasted partridge to her, but while she ate it, he died. To honor the generous old man, the Great Spirit grew a wonderful food in the field where he was buried. This food was corn, and it was named Mondomin after the kind old hunter.

The Indians of Massachusetts held many festivals to thank the gods for providing for them. An important festival called the Feast of the Green Corn celebrated the first ripening of the corn. During the week-long festival the Indians feasted, prayed, sang and danced, and played games and sports.

One sport enjoyed by the Indians was like soccer. Goalposts were set up as far as a mile apart. Two teams, often from two different villages, tried to kick a small deerskin ball into their opponents' goal. These games often lasted for several days and were very brutal. One tribe, the Massachusett, made sure that no one could hold a grudge against individual players. For each contest they painted their faces a different way.

A popular game among the Indians of Massachusetts was known as Hubbub. It was a dice game, played with several bones or beans with markings on them. The game earned its name from the way the players cried, "Hub, hub, hub!" while throwing the dice. The betting was so heavy at Hubbub that players were known to return home naked after a game because they had gambled away their clothes! Other sports and games enjoyed by the Indians included swimming, archery contests, and footraces.

War club

Painting entitled *Fight Between the Dakotahs and the Alconquins*

Although the first Europeans to reach Massachusetts usually described the Indians as peaceful, the tribes sometimes fought one another. For example, the Massachusett tribe sometimes warred against the Wampanoags of southeastern Massachusetts and the Narragansetts of Rhode Island. Indian weapons included stone-tipped clubs called tomahawks and also bows and arrows. Thanks to archery contests and hunting, many braves could hit a moving enemy at a distance of more than a hundred feet.

The Indians' approach to warfare was much different from that of the whites across the Atlantic Ocean. Europeans had formal rules for waging war. Battles were fought in open fields in broad daylight, prisoners were supposed to be well treated, and surprise attacks were considered cowardly. The Indians believed that the enemy should be destroyed with the fewest possible losses to one's own side, which was why they made "sneak attacks." Instead of taking prisoners, the Indians sometimes killed every person in an enemy village so that no one could take revenge on them later.

The Indians and the Europeans also had conflicting ideas about land. The Europeans believed that land could be bought and sold. To the Indians, land was like the air—something that could not be owned. Differing views about land ownership were to help create clashes between the Indians and the Europeans once the first years of friendship ended.

The names of the first Europeans to arrive in Massachusetts are unknown. Although no artifacts have been found to prove it, some historians think that around A.D. 1000 Leif Ericsson and other Vikings (Scandinavians) reached Massachusetts. One of the first known

Leif Ericsson statue carved by Alexander Calder.

Dramatic painting showing Leif Ericsson's discovery of North America.

explorers in Massachusetts was a Portuguese named Miguel Cortereal, whose ship was wrecked on the coast in 1502. At the mouth of the Taunton River in Bristol County is an eleven-foot-long granite rock known as Dighton Rock. Carved on it are the words "M. Cortereal 1511 V. Dei Dux Ind.," which is Latin for "M. Cortereal 1511 by God's grace the leader of the Indians." From this, historians think that Cortereal lived with the Indians for a time and was made their chief.

Because so many European explorers sailed to so many places during the 1500s, that century is called the Age of Discovery. During those years men from Italy, France, Spain, Portugal, and England sailed along, and sometimes landed on, the Massachusetts coast. Some came to trade with the Indians, others were on fishing expeditions, while still others wanted to learn about the land so that colonies could be built there. By the year 1600, hundreds of European sailors were familiar with the Massachusetts coast and its Indians.

In 1602 the English explorer Bartholomew Gosnold, with about thirty men, sailed the small

Explorers from Europe came to trade with the Indians.

ship *Concord* from England to the northeastern coast of what is now the United States. Searching for sassafras tree roots, which were thought to have medicinal value, Gosnold moved down the coast from Maine to Rhode Island. While in Massachusetts, Gosnold landed on a long peninsula shaped like a fishing hook. Because of all the codfish his men caught near that peninsula, Gosnold named it Cape Cod, which is still its name today.

Artist's reconstruction of Gosnold's fort.

Continuing southward, Gosnold landed on an island just four miles off Cape Cod. He named this island Martha's Vineyard—"Martha" after his daughter and "Vineyard" because of all the grapevines growing there. Gosnold also explored and named the nearby Elizabeth Islands. On one of the Elizabeths, now called Cuttyhunk Island, he and his men built a house and a fort. They also planted "Wheat, Barley, Oats, and Pease, which in fourteene daies were sprung up nine inches and more," according to John Brereton, a sailor who kept a journal of the expedition.

Besides gathering sassafras, Gosnold traded for furs with the Indians, who were "exceeding courteous [and] gentle of disposition," according to Brereton. Bartholomew Gosnold liked Massachusetts so much that he planned to leave twenty men there to build a colony. Dwindling supplies wrecked this plan, however. After sailing south to what is now Rhode Island's Narragansett Bay, the men returned to England with their cargo of sassafras and furs.

The stories Gosnold and his crew told about the land in Massachusetts stirred up interest. In 1606 two companies were formed by English merchants who wanted to profit from colonizing America. One, the London Company, sent John Smith, Bartholomew Gosnold, and others to settle in what is now Virginia. In 1607 they founded Jamestown, the first permanent English settlement in America.

The king of England gave the other company, called the Plymouth Company, the right to colonize the northeastern coast of America from

Jamestown has been built again to show people what the first colony in America looked like.

what is now Delaware up to Maine. In 1607 (the same year that the Jamestown Colony was founded in Virginia), English colonists sent by the Plymouth Company set up Popham Plantation on the coast of Maine. However, a cold winter and a fire forced the Maine colonists to leave their

20

settlement after just a year. Since the Jamestown colonists were having trouble surviving in Virginia despite its mild climate, the English figured that building a permanent settlement to the north was nearly impossible.

Meanwhile, explorers continued to map the Massachusetts region. France had begun to settle Canada in about 1604. In 1605 and again in 1606 the Frenchman Samuel de Champlain sailed down from Canada as far south as Massachusetts. On these voyages Champlain explored and mapped the New England coast. A few years later,

Woodcut showing Champlain fighting Indians

Some Indian tribes helped the explorers fight other Indian tribes.

John Smith, the man who had led the founding of the Jamestown Colony, did the same.

In 1609 Smith was seriously hurt in a gunpowder explosion in Virginia and had to return to England. He had fallen in love with America, however, and yearned to return. In 1614 Smith was asked to go to America on a fishing and fur-trading expedition. While on this trip, John Smith explored much of the coast of the northeastern United States. Smith named the region New England and made the best maps of the area up to that time. The name Massachusetts was used for the first time on Smith's maps. He named it after the Massachusett Indian tribe. The word *Massachusett* is thought to mean "the place of the great hill" and probably refers to the Great Blue Hill south of present-day Boston.

In 1616 John Smith published *A Description of New England*. He gave his readers a detailed account of the region's land, people, plants, and animals. Smith called Massachusetts "the paradise of all those parts," and said that "could I have but means to transport a colony, I would

Captain John Smith

Maps drawn by John Smith were used by the Pilgrims.

rather live here [in Massachusetts] than anywhere."

Among those who read John Smith's writings were some people who had fled England because of religious persecution and were living in The Netherlands. When they left Europe and headed for Massachusetts they became known to history as the Pilgrims.

English soldiers stop the Pilgrims from fleeing to The Netherlands.

Chapter II

The Coming of the Pilgrims

Being thus arrived in a good harbor and brought safe to land [at Cape Cod, Massachusetts], they fell upon their knees & blessed ye God of heaven, who had brought them over ye vast & furious ocean, and delivered them from all ye periles & miseries thereof, againe to set their feete on ye firme and stable earth, their proper elemente.

From Of Plimoth Plantation, *by the Pilgrim leader William Bradford*

King James I

During the early years of the seventeenth century, people in England could not worship as they pleased. James I had become king in 1603. He believed that monarchs ruled by divine right, meaning their power was God-given. James ordered all his subjects to follow a single religion, the Church of England. Those who did not belong to this church or who criticized it risked punishment.

Nevertheless, many people did not like the Church of England. One group believed that the Church of England had too many rituals and that people were appointed to high church offices for

In the 1600s, upper-class Englishmen wore fancy, colorful clothes. But not the Puritan man. He wore plain black as another sign of his belief in simple things.

political, rather than for religious, reasons. They were called Puritans. They wanted to purify religion by making services simpler and by focusing more on the Bible. Most Puritans did not leave the Church of England. They wanted to change and improve it from within.

Some Puritans, however, broke away completely from the Church of England. Because they had separated themselves from the church, such people were called Separatists. Because it was a serious crime against the state to belong to a Separatist church in England, the Puritan Separatists held secret services.

One Puritan Separatist group, led by William Brewster, met in the village of Scrooby in central England. In 1607 the Scrooby Separatists came to the attention of King James I. Because of their religious beliefs, the Scrooby Separatists had their jobs and property taken away. Some were even thrown into prison.

The village of Scrooby

The city of Leiden in The Netherlands

To escape this persecution, in 1608 most of the Scrooby Separatists left their homes and fled to The Netherlands, which offered more freedom of religion than any other European nation. By 1609 they had settled in the city of Leiden, where they remained for eleven years. As they had hoped, the Separatists from Scrooby were able to practice their religion in peace in Leiden. Other Separatists from England joined them there.

As years passed, the Separatists found that life in The Netherlands had certain drawbacks. Many of them had trouble earning a living, partly because of the language barrier and partly because some Dutch people resented having to compete with them for jobs. Also, the Separatists realized that their children were beginning to consider themselves Dutch rather than English. The Separatists in Leiden began to look for a place where they could earn more money while preserving their English heritage.

At this time, reports on New England written by Captain John Smith and others were reaching Europe. Although Smith had painted an overly rosy picture about the region, the Separatists from Scrooby knew that survival in New England would be difficult. Reports from the only permanent English settlement in America, the Jamestown Colony, proved this. Of the first one thousand colonists who went to Jamestown after its founding in 1607, all but sixty had died of hunger, disease, and other hardships by 1610.

The Separatists from Scrooby had already risked much for the sake of their beliefs, and some now decided to take another chance. William Bradford,* one of their leaders, described in his book *Of Plimoth Plantation* how the decision to sail to America was finally made:

> *It was answered [to those who thought they should not go], that all great & honourable actions are accompanied with great difficulties, and must be both enterprised and overcome with answerable courages. It was granted ye dangers were great, but not desperate; the difficulties were many, but not invincible. . . . All of them, through ye help of God, by fortitude and patience, might either be borne, or overcome.*

* For more information about William Bradford see page 53

King James gave the Puritans the right to build a colony in North America.

When King James heard that some of the Scrooby Separatists wanted to go to America, he asked how they would support themselves there. Learning that they would probably do so by fishing, the king (who was glad to be rid of them) is said to have answered: "Very good. It was the apostles' own calling." The Separatists from Scrooby were given the right to colonize land

30

north of the Jamestown Colony. They were advised by English officials to settle near the mouth of the Hudson River at what is now New York City.

After getting financial help from some wealthy London merchants, several dozen Separatists who were bound for America sailed to England. There they were joined by several dozen non-Separatists, who also wanted to go to America.

The house in Plymouth, England where the Pilgrims were entertained before sailing to America

The voyagers started out in two ships—the *Mayflower* and a smaller vessel, the *Speedwell.* The *Speedwell* was "leakie as a seive," according to one traveler, and twice had to return to England, accompanied by the *Mayflower,* for repairs. Finally, the *Speedwell* was abandoned and all 102 men, women, and children who were going to America boarded the *Mayflower.* On September 16, 1620, the *Mayflower* headed out to sea from Plymouth, England. It was bound for the coast of America, three thousand miles away.

The people who came to America aboard the *Mayflower* are usually called Pilgrims. It is believed that this name was first used by William Bradford, one of the group's leaders. In his first-hand account, *Of Plimoth Plantation,* Bradford wrote that the voyagers "knew they were pilgrims"

Pilgrims leave England.

when they set out on their dangerous journey. He noted that he took the word *pilgrims* from chapter 11 of the New Testament book Epistle to the Hebrews, in which it is stated:

> . . . *they were strangers and pilgrims on the earth. . . .*
> *But now they desire a better country. . . .*

By today's standards the *Mayflower* was tiny for an oceangoing ship. It was only about ninety feet long. The Atlantic Ocean was stormy during the two-month-long autumn crossing, and as the

Opposite page: The *Mayflower* left Plymouth, England in 1620

32

little ship was tossed about many of the passengers became seasick. Yet even though they were poorly fed, cold, wet, and cramped together, all but one of the Pilgrims were alive when they sighted Cape Cod, Massachusetts at dawn of November 19, 1620. During the Atlantic crossing Elizabeth Hopkins had given birth to a child whom she and her husband named Oceanus, so the number of Pilgrims to reach Massachusetts still stood at 102.

Massachusetts was north of the area where the Pilgrims had expected to settle, so Captain Christopher Jones headed the *Mayflower* south toward the mouth of the Hudson River. However, the little vessel was fighting fierce winds and waves. There was danger of becoming ship-wrecked on the rocks along Cape Cod. The Pilgrims met and decided to stay in Massachusetts rather than risk the trip south. Captain Jones then sailed the *Mayflower* into the shelter of Cape Cod's Provincetown Harbor. Once there, the Pilgrims knelt down on the ship's deck and thanked God for safely guiding them across the ocean.

The Pilgrim leaders feared that disagreements would ruin their chances for a successful colony.

Some of the non-Separatists were already threatening to do whatever they wanted once they reached shore. To make sure that everyone would work together, the adult male passengers on the *Mayflower* made an agreement while the ship sat in Provincetown Harbor. This pact is called the Mayflower Compact. It was the first agreement for self-government put into effect in what is now the United States.

This painting by E. Moran shows the Pilgrims signing the Mayflower Compact

Signatures of some of the Pilgrims

Statue of William Bradford

The Mayflower Compact was signed by forty-one adult men. (At the time, women rarely were allowed to take part in legal matters.) The original Mayflower Compact has been lost, but William Bradford gave the text of it in his book, *Of Plimoth Plantation:**

In ye name of God, Amen. We whose names are underwritten, the loyall subjects of our dread soveraigne Lord, King James, by ye grace of God, of Great Britaine, Franc, & c., haveing undertaken, for ye glorie of God, and advancemente of ye Christian faith, and honour of our king and countrie, a voyage to plant ye first colonie in ye Northerne parts of Virginia, doe by these presents solemnly & mutualy in ye presence of God, and one of another, covenant & combine our selves togeather into a civill body politick, for our better ordering & preservation & furtherance of ye ends aforesaid; and by vertue hearof to enacte, constitute, and frame such just & equall lawes, ordinances, acts, constitutions, & offices, from time to time, as shall be thought most meete & convenient for ye generall good of ye Colonie, unto which we promise all due submission and obedience. In witnes whereof we have hereunder subscribed our names at Cap-Codd ye 11. of November [November 21, by the calendar now used], in ye year of ye raigne of our soveraigne lord King James, of England, France, & Ireland ye eighteenth, and of Scotland ye fiftie fourth. Ano: Dom. 1620.

Besides making this agreement, the men also chose John Carver, "a man godly & well approved

* For more information about *Of Plimoth Plantation* see pages 170 to 172

amongst them" (according to William Bradford), as their first governor.

The Pilgrims then had to decide where exactly to build their colony. Miles Standish, a non-Separatist who had been hired as a military expert, led the first exploring trip. When Standish's men brought some corn back to the *Mayflower*, the people stared at it in amazement. None of them had ever seen this plant before. Several days later a child was born on the *Mayflower*. Since the Pilgrims still were looking for a place to settle, the baby's parents named him Peregrine, a Latin name that means "wanderer." Peregrine White, who was the first English child born in New England, lived to be eighty-three years old.

Miles Standish

The Pilgrims explored the coast along Cape Cod Bay for a month. In mid-December Miles Standish, Governor John Carver, and William Bradford led an expedition. The men were camped near a little barricade they had built on the beach at modern-day North Eastham on Cape Cod. Suddenly Indians attacked. Fortunately for the Englishmen, they were able to grab their muskets and drive them off.

Peregrine White's cradle

Miles Standish
explores Plymouth.

Plymouth Rock

A few hours later the Englishmen were out in their small boat when a blinding snowstorm forced them to take refuge on an island in Plymouth Harbor. The next day the weary travelers rested because it was the Sabbath. On the day after that, December 21, 1620, they rowed their little boat ashore to the place John Smith had named Plymouth (after Plymouth, England) on his map of the Massachusetts coast. According to tradition, the exploring party that came ashore at Plymouth stepped on a granite boulder now called Plymouth Rock.

Once ashore, the explorers were delighted to find a clear stream and a high hill that would make a good site for a fort. They also spotted some abandoned cornfields. The fields had belonged to the small Patuxet tribe, which had been wiped out (except for one survivor) in a smallpox epidemic.

The explorers returned to the *Mayflower* and told the others about the spot they had found. On December 26, 1620, the *Mayflower* crossed Cape Cod Bay and landed at Plymouth. When the other Pilgrims saw Plymouth, they agreed that it was a good place to settle.

The Pilgrim's land in Plymouth, Massachusetts.

The Pilgrim's worked together to build their colony.

Late December was a bad time of year to start building a colony in Massachusetts. On days when the weather permitted, the Pilgrims chopped down trees and sawed them into logs. They used the logs to construct a common house (a building for group activities), a combination church-fort, and a few small houses where the colonists would live.

Conditions were terrible for the Pilgrims during their first winter at Plymouth. The men who were building the town had to brave the cold and the snow. Those still living aboard the *Mayflower* had it almost as bad. Before December ended half a dozen Pilgrims had died of disease—possibly typhus or scurvy. Each month during that winter, disease killed another ten or twelve people. By winter's end, only about fifty of the colonists were still alive.

By the early spring of 1621 Indians had gathered near Plymouth. Each day they came a little nearer—whether out of curiosity or as preparation for an attack the Pilgrims did not know. The few surviving men were in the common house discussing what to do if the Indians attacked when Samoset suddenly walked into Plymouth saying, "Welcome, Englishmen!"

Samoset, who had learned English from fishermen in Maine, was so friendly that he eased the colonists' fear of Indians. He told the Pilgrims about the land and people of Massachusetts, and then asked them if they had any beer. They had none, but they did share their dinner of duck, biscuits, cheese, and pudding with him. Samoset spent the night in the house of Elizabeth and Stephen Hopkins, the parents of Oceanus.

The next day Samoset left Plymouth, but he soon returned with five other Indians. These five brought with them some tools which had been stolen from the Pilgrims' hiding place in the woods. The return of their tools greatly cheered the Pilgrims, for it showed that the Indians

Squanto comes to
Plymouth Colony.

wanted to be friendly. The five other Indians sang
and danced for the Pilgrims and then left, but
Samoset once again stayed the night with his new
friends. Before saying good-bye, Samoset said
that next time he would bring Squanto,* an Indian
who knew English even better than himself
because he had been to England.

As promised, the next day Samoset returned
with Squanto, who was the sole survivor of the
Patuxet tribe. Samoset and Squanto explained
that Chief Massasoit* was nearby and wanted to

* For more information about Squanto and Massasoit see page 52

42

meet the Pilgrims. A peaceful meeting with Massasoit was important, for he was chief of the Wampanoags. His tribe controlled southeastern Massachusetts, including the spot where Plymouth was located. Squanto went back and forth between the Indians and the Pilgrim leaders to arrange a meeting. Finally, Massasoit and twenty of his braves put their weapons aside and marched into Plymouth. Captain Standish escorted Massasoit into a house, and there the Indian chief met John Carver, the Plymouth Colony governor.

The Native Americans had many reasons to dislike the English. For one thing, the English had built a settlement without asking permission. Also, Massasoit and his people knew that Indians had been mistreated by other Europeans in the past. They had been tricked in trade, carried off to Europe as prisoners, and sometimes shot without cause. For all these reasons, it would not have been surprising if Massasoit had ordered the Pilgrims to leave.

Instead, Governor Carver was pleased to find that Massasoit wanted to be friends. Some historians think that Massasoit wanted the powerful English as allies in case of war with

The Pilgrims signed a peace treaty with Massasoit.

other tribes. Others say that Massasoit was a generous man who did not mind sharing the land with the English. Whatever the reason, Carver and Massasoit exchanged kisses and shared a drink of brandy as tokens of friendship. After that, the two leaders went to work.

Carver and Massasoit agreed that their people would not carry weapons in each other's presence. Also, each group would aid the other in case of attack by a third party. Massasoit then took out his tobacco, and the two leaders smoked the peace pipe. The peace treaty that John Carver and Massasoit agreed to on that spring day in 1621 lasted for more than fifty years.

Squanto's friendship proved to be just as important as Massasoit's to the Pilgrims. Since his own people were dead, Squanto adopted the English as his family. About the time that the *Mayflower* sailed back to England in early spring of 1621, Squanto showed the Pilgrims the best fishing spots. Squanto also taught them how to plant corn and how to use dead fish to fertilize the ground.

Squanto taught the Pilgrims how to plant corn.

Drawing of Plymouth Colony made from the Pilgrims' written descriptions of the town

One day when the corn was still being planted, Governor Carver came home from the fields complaining of a headache. He lay down, fell into a coma, and died several days later. William Bradford, whose book has provided so much information about the Plymouth Colony, was then chosen as governor. Under Bradford's direction the Pilgrims continued to build. By the end of the summer of 1621 Plymouth was a town with streets, houses, and several public buildings.

At harvesttime, the Pilgrims found that the seeds they had brought from England for such crops as wheat and peas had done poorly. However, the corn grown under Squanto's supervision was beautiful. Massachusetts was a paradise to the Pilgrims in that autumn of 1621. Hunters bagged deer, ducks, and turkeys. The colonists gathered wild grapes, which they made into a sweet wine. In addition, a supply of cod and bass was left from the summer's fishing trips. The Pilgrims were so happy about all this abundance that they decided to have a thanksgiving celebration.

The first Thanksgiving

Governor Bradford invited Massasoit and about ninety of his Indians to the three-day celebration, held sometime in the fall of 1621. The Indians brought deer meat and wild turkeys to the feast, while the colonists provided fish, geese, ducks, corn bread, and succotash (corn and beans cooked together). This was the first thanksgiving feast held by the English in what is now the United States. Later, the Pilgrims continued to hold thanksgiving celebrations in years of good harvests. This tradition grew into the Thanksgiving holiday now held across the United States on the fourth Thursday of every November.

Around the time of the first thanksgiving feast, the *Fortune* arrived in Plymouth Harbor. Aboard the ship were thirty-five new English colonists, some of them relatives and friends of the Pilgrims. The *Fortune* also carried an official paper called a charter from the newly formed Council for New England, the group now in charge of leasing New England lands. The charter stated that the Plymouth Colony could remain where it was.

Soon after the *Fortune* sailed away, Governor William Bradford found a small package outside the door to his house. Inside was a bundle of arrows wrapped in a rattlesnake skin. Squanto

The Massachusetts Charter

explained that this was a threatening message from Canonicus, chief of the powerful Narragansetts of Rhode Island.

Although the Pilgrims had only about fifty armed men and Canonicus commanded thousands of warriors, Bradford answered the challenge. He stuffed the snakeskin with bullets and powder as a symbol that the Pilgrims were ready for war. Squanto delivered the package to Canonicus. The chief was so upset by the Pilgrims' boldness that he returned the bullets and gunpowder as a sign that he no longer

The Pilgrims traded with the Indians.

wanted to fight. Nevertheless, the Plymouth colonists soon built palisades (tall wooden fences) around their town for protection.

Within a year of Plymouth's founding, it was apparent that the colony was going to last. One key to the Plymouth Colony's success was the fact that it had been settled mainly by families who wanted good, permanent homes. Because they had come to stay, these people did not go off looking for gold, as members of other short-lived colonies had done. Instead, they turned to farming and fishing, which allowed them to build a stable community.

Besides supporting themselves, the Pilgrims had to repay their debt to the Englishmen who had helped finance the colony. To do this the Pilgrims traded for furs with the Indians, then shipped the valuable furs back to England. The Pilgrims eventually did repay their debt, but it took them nearly thirty years to do so.

During the 1620s ships brought more Separatists as well as "strangers" to Plymouth, and the town slowly grew. In 1627 the colonists developed a system by which twenty acres of land were granted to each person in the colony, meaning that a family of six would receive 120 acres. The offering of land attracted even more families to Massachusetts. As the Plymouth region filled up some of the colonists moved to outlying areas. Towns founded during the 1630s included Duxbury (1632) and Scituate (1633) to the north of Plymouth, and Barnstable (1638) and Yarmouth (1639) to the east on Cape Cod.

By 1640 the Plymouth Colony was made up of eight towns that were home to 2,500 persons. By that time a second group had come to Massachusetts to build another colony—the Massachusetts Bay Colony.

SQUANTO (?-1622)

Born somewhere in New England in the late 1500s, Squanto was a member of the small Patuxet tribe of Massachusetts' Plymouth region. The few facts known about Squanto suggest that he lived an adventurous but tragic life.

In 1615 an English sea captain kidnapped Squanto and twenty-six other Indians from the Massachusetts coast and took them to Málaga, Spain, where they were sold into slavery. Squanto managed to escape and make his way to London. After several years in England's largest city, Squanto was taken to Newfoundland, Canada, where an English sea captain arranged to use him as a guide and interpreter on a trading trip to Massachusetts. When Squanto finally reached his home in the Plymouth region in 1619, he found that every other member of the Patuxet tribe had died of smallpox, which the Indians had caught from the English explorers.

Squanto, the last surviving Patuxet Indian, went to live with his neighbors, the Wampanoags. Several months after the *Mayflower* arrived at Plymouth in late 1620, Samoset introduced Squanto to the Pilgrims. Squanto taught the Pilgrims how to farm and fish, and was so vital to the colony's success that William Bradford called him "a spetiall instrument sent of God for [the Pilgrims'] good beyond their expectation."

Squanto lived with the Pilgrims for the last two years of his life. Late in 1622 he was serving as guide and interpreter on William Bradford's trading expedition to Cape Cod when he came down with a high fever. Shortly before he died at Chatham Harbor on Cape Cod, Squanto said that his greatest wish was to go to the Englishmen's heaven.

MASSASOIT (1580?-1661)

Massasoit, whose birthplace is unknown, was the chief of the Wampanoags of southeastern Massachusetts. At a time when his warriors greatly outnumbered the Pilgrims, Massasoit agreed to a peace treaty with the English in 1621. As he had promised, he kept the peace for the last forty years of his life.

In turn, the Pilgrims proved to be good friends to Massasoit. They invited him and some of his braves to their Thanksgiving in the fall of 1621. After the bountiful feast, Massasoit is said to have told the Pilgrims, "The Great Spirit surely must love his white children best."

In 1623 Massasoit sent word that he was very ill and expected to die. A Pilgrim leader, Edward Winslow, went to the great chief to see what he could do. It turned out that Massasoit had overeaten and was suffering from a chief-sized stomachache. Winslow gave him one of the Pilgrims' homemade remedies, and the chief soon recovered. The grateful Massasoit informed the Pilgrims that another tribe was about to attack the town of Weymouth. This information helped the English prevent the attack.

Massasoit died at about the age of eighty and has been remembered ever since as one of the great peacekeepers of colonial times. His son, Metacomet, was a much different kind of man who pledged himself to the destruction of the English.

WILLIAM BRADFORD (1590-1657)

Born in the country village of Austerfield, England, William Bradford was just a year old when his father died, and only seven when his mother died. The orphaned boy was sent to live with two uncles in Austerfield.

When William reached his early teens he began walking sixteen miles each Sunday to attend a Puritan church in a nearby town. Upon learning of this, his uncles forbade him to attend any more Puritan services. Young William Bradford followed his conscience when it came to religion, however. In 1606 he upset his family even more by quitting the Church of England and joining the Separatist church at Scrooby.

At eighteen, William Bradford left England with other members of the Scrooby congregation and settled in The Netherlands. During his twelve years in that country, Bradford worked as a weaver and was married to a young woman named Dorothy May. In 1620 Dorothy and William Bradford left Europe forever when they sailed to America on the *Mayflower.*

William Bradford was involved in one of the first tragedies to befall the Pilgrims in Massachusetts. Returning from the trip on which he and a few others had located Plymouth, Bradford learned that his wife was dead. Somehow Dorothy Bradford had gone over the side of the *Mayflower* as it sat in Provincetown Harbor. Whether her drowning was an accident or suicide was never determined.

William Bradford dedicated the rest of his life to the Plymouth Colony's welfare. He helped build the town, and in April of 1621 he was elected governor of the colony when John Carver died. Bradford was so hardworking and fair that he was elected governor again and again. In fact, Bradford was governor continually between 1621 and 1657, except for five years when he insisted on being relieved. William Bradford's book, *Of Plimoth Plantation,* is the main historical account of the colony's early years.

Puritan prayer meeting

Chapter III

The Coming of the Puritans

. . . we must knit together in this work [the founding of a new colony in Massachusetts], as one man. We must entertain each other in brotherly affection. . . . We must delight in each other; make others' conditions our own, rejoice together, mourn together, labor and suffer together, always having before our eyes our commission and community in the work, as members of the same body. . . .

From "A Modell of Christian Charity," written at sea by Puritan leader John Winthrop in 1630

During the late 1620s conditions were still bad for Puritans in England. In 1625 Charles I, the son of James I, became king of England. Anti-Puritan like his father, Charles I stripped Puritans of their property, removed them from their jobs, and in some cases imprisoned them. In the late 1620s a large group of Puritans asked King Charles for permission to form a colony in the Massachusetts Bay region, about forty miles north of the Plymouth Colony. Glad to be rid of them, King Charles gave his permission.

King Charles I

John Endecott

John Winthrop

In 1628 the Puritan leader John Endecott (1588?-1665) led an advance party of about fifty Puritans to the shores of Massachusetts Bay. They settled at a place the Indians called Naumkeag (meaning "safe haven"), and there they laid out a town they named Salem. Salem was the first town in the Massachusetts Bay Colony, which was completely separate from the Plymouth Colony.

When word reached England that Salem really was a safe haven for their people, more Puritans sailed there. The largest exodus was made under the leadership of London lawyer John Winthrop (1588-1649), who was to be the new colony's first governor. In the spring of 1630 Winthrop led an eleven-ship fleet carrying a thousand Puritans out of England.

The movement of all those people under Winthrop was a well-planned event. The Puritans brought with them everything needed to build a successful colony. Packed into the ships were large quantities of oatmeal, butter, cheese, sugar, bacon, and other foods. Also on board were horses, cows, chickens, goats, pigs, tools, nails, extra clothes, blankets, cooking pots, guns,

Governor Winthrop's fleet (from the left, the *Talbot*, the *Arbella*, and the *Jewell*) in Boston Harbor

ammunition, and—last but definitely not least—books.

There were several major differences between the Pilgrims who had founded Plymouth in 1620 and the Puritans who crossed the ocean in spring of 1630. The most important difference concerned religion.

The Pilgrims were Puritans, too. But what made the Pilgrims of 1620 special was the fact that they were Separatists—people who had rebelled against the Church of England and left it altogether. The Puritans of 1630 were not Separatists, but instead wanted to purify the Church of England from within.

The early Pilgrims for the most part were poor, not very educated, but open-minded. They believed that people should be allowed to live and worship as they chose, which was one reason why they got along well with the Indians. The Puritans, on the other hand, believed that God had chosen them to teach the world how to live and worship. They had little patience for opinions that differed from theirs. They were also wealthier than the Pilgrims. In fact, their well-stocked fleet had cost the equivalent of more than $100 million in 1980s U.S. money. In addition, the Puritans were highly educated.

The Puritan fleet took more than two months to cross the Atlantic Ocean. In June and July of 1630 the ships arrived one by one at the Massachusetts coast near Salem. The Puritans were rowed in small boats into Salem, where the earlier settlers already were living.

The Puritans were too numerous to settle as one group in Salem or in any other single place. Their charter entitled them to make their homes

The first church in New England

in a large area around Massachusetts Bay. Soon after their arrival, groups of Puritans left Salem and began building settlements at Lynn, Dorchester, Medford, and Watertown. About eight hundred of the Puritans followed Governor Winthrop to a spot near the mouth of the Charles River, where they founded a town called Charlestown (part of present-day Boston).

Soon after arriving in Charlestown, Governor Winthrop and his eight hundred followers discovered that the area had a shortage of fresh drinking water, so they searched for a nearby spot to build a town. Just to the south across the

Charles River, a man named William Blackstone was living in a cottage by himself at present-day Beacon Hill. Blackstone spent his time tending his orchards, trading with the Indians, and reading his library of nearly two hundred books. When he learned that a large group of Puritans needed a place to build a town, Blackstone invited Winthrop and his followers to settle near him. In summer of 1630 they crossed the Charles River and began building their town near Blackstone's home. They named it Boston after the English town from which many of them had come.

Although several hundred people died in the Massachusetts Bay Colony during the harsh

A distant view of the Boston area where, between 1630 and 1640, more than ten thousand Puritans settled.

Typical New England
school

winter of 1630-31, John Winthrop wrote to
England that Massachusetts was a wonderful
place where Puritans could worship in peace.
Between 1630 and 1640, more than ten thousand
additional Puritans sailed to the colony and
settled in Boston* and the other growing towns.
They also helped to found new towns, including
Newtowne (which changed its name to Cambridge
in 1638), Ipswich, and Salisbury.

The Massachusetts Puritans valued education
highly. They believed a person needed to be
educated in order to study the Bible. Their love for
learning helped them accomplish many
educational "firsts." In 1635 they founded the
Boston Latin School, the first public school in
what is now the United States. In 1647 the

* For more information about Boston see pages 173 and 174

Massachusetts Bay Colony passed a law requiring each town of fifty or more families to maintain a school that was partly supported by taxes. This was the beginning of the public school system in America.

Puritan children spent up to ten hours per day in school. Religious lessons and reading were the two most important subjects. The Puritans believed that children were "better whipt, than damn'd," and those few who were naughty in school were brought into line by the teacher's birch rod. Girls were taught only to read and write, but boys went on to study a variety of subjects. By age fourteen many Massachusetts Bay Colony boys knew Latin and Greek and were ready to enter the new college that had been founded at Newtowne (now Cambridge) in the fall of 1636.

Harvard College

This college was called the College of Newtowne when it opened in 1638, but a year later its name was changed to Havard. The renaming was done out of respect for a deceased minister named John Harvard, who had given a large sum of money and a library of many volumes to the school. Harvard was the first college in what is now the United States.

The Harvard College library was the first library in England's American colonies, and today is the oldest library in the United States. The first printing press in the American colonies was set up in Cambridge, by a printer named Stephen Daye. In 1640 Stephen and his son, Matthew Daye, printed *The Bay Psalm Book*, the first English-language book to be published in America.

Stephen Daye's printing press.

Despite their love for learning, the Puritans did not like people who did not do things their way. The Massachusetts Bay Colony was a theocracy—a state in which laws and government are based on religion. Those who disagreed with or disobeyed the Puritan religious leaders were considered lawbreakers. For example, people who cursed or missed church might be fined, publicly whipped, or placed in the town's pillory. Those

The pillory (left) and the stocks (right) were used to publicly punish people who had broken the laws of the Puritans.

who disagreed with the leaders on religious matters were banished or even executed.

Roger Williams (1603?-1683), a young clergyman living in Salem, disagreed strongly with the Puritans on religious issues. Williams had the boldness to preach that everyone had the right to worship as he or she wished. He further angered Puritan leaders by saying that the Indians were the true owners of Massachusetts land.

Painting dramatizing Roger Williams' escape to the Indians

In the fall of 1635 Roger Williams was found guilty of spreading "newe and dangerous opinions" and ordered by the legislature to leave the Massachusetts Bay Colony by the following spring. When Williams continued to express his "newe and dangerous opinions," the order was made for his arrest and return to England. To avoid this, Williams escaped into the woods, where he and his wife spent the winter with the Indians in their huts.

In 1636 Roger Williams bought some land from the Indians at the head of Narragansett Bay in what is now Rhode Island. There Williams established a settlement he called Providence because he felt that God had provided the place for his followers and himself. Providence was the first permanent non-Indian settlement in what is now Rhode Island. It was also the first American town to guarantee religious freedom to all people.

Anne Hutchinson

Other people also founded new settlements after being forced to leave the Massachusetts Bay Colony. In 1637 Anne Hutchinson (1591-1643) was banished because of her religious views. She, her family, and some followers went to Rhode Island, where in 1638 they founded the settlement which became Portsmouth. Several of the families who had left with Hutchinson then founded

Newport, Rhode Island, in 1639. Many people who fled the Massachusetts Bay Colony because of religious intolerance became the early settlers of Connecticut, New Hampshire, and Maine. Some even went to live in the more tolerant Plymouth Colony to the south.

Meanwhile, back in the Massachusetts Bay Colony, the Puritans still were trying to convert everyone to their way of thinking. The Indians were among their main targets. During the 1640s the Massachusetts Bay Puritans began sending out missionaries to the Indians. Although one Indian group said they were not foolish enough to trade their several dozen gods for just one Christian god, the missionaries did convert many Native Americans to the Puritan faith.

The leading Puritan missionary was John Eliot (1604-1690), a teacher and minister who converted hundreds of Indians. Eliot learned Algonquian so that he could talk to the Indians in their own language. He also worked out a written language for Algonquian and spent twelve years translating the Bible into it. Eliot's Indian Bible was the first Bible in any language printed in the American colonies.

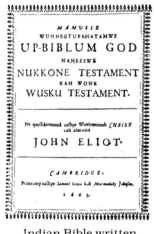

Indian Bible written by John Eliot

Engraving showing
John Eliot preaching
to the Indians

Although the missionaries wanted to share their religion with the Indians, they did not want to live with the Native Americans. For this reason, Eliot built separate villages for the "praying Indians"—those who had become Christians. The first such "praying town" was Natick, founded near Boston by Eliot in 1651. Eliot eventually helped build fourteen "praying towns," which were home to about four thousand Christianized Indians.

Indian church in the wilderness

Unlike John Eliot, many Massachusetts Bay Colony people did not think of Indians as human beings. These people cheated the Indians in trades, including deals that cost the Native Americans their homelands. By the mid-1600s, the good feeling between the colonists and the Indians in the Plymouth Colony was also eroding. To make matters worse, in 1637 the Massachusetts Bay Puritans and the Plymouth Pilgrims had taken part in the burning alive of seven hundred Pequot in Connecticut during the Pequot War.

True to his word, Massasoit kept peace with the Plymouth colonists all his life, but a year after his death in 1661 a different kind of chief came to power. He was the son of Massasoit and his name was Metacomet (1639?-1676), but the English called him King Philip. Metacomet hated the English for having taken so much land. Afraid that his people would one day have no place to call home, Metacomet decided that the Indians must drive all the colonists out of New England.

Plymouth Colony officials realized that Metacomet was a threat to them and arrested him several times. After one arrest in 1671, Metacomet and his people were made to turn over their firearms. When he tried to get the guns back, Metacomet learned that officials had given the weapons away to their fellow English colonists.

King Philip

"My father gave them what they asked," Metacomet said bitterly about this. "They have had townships and whole Indian kingdoms for a few blankets, hoes, and flattering words. But they are not content—the white man's throat is wide."

At about this time Metacomet realized that to beat the English he needed more warriors than his people, the Wampanoags, could provide. Metacomet convinced large numbers of Narragansett, Nipmuc, Pocasset, and Sakonnet Indians to fight alongside the Wampanoags. These allies gathered near his headquarters at Mount Hope (now Bristol), Rhode Island.

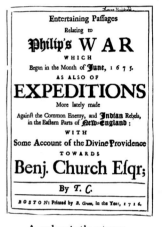

A colonist's story about the war with the Indians

In the summer of 1675 a white man shot and wounded an Indian in the Plymouth Colony town of Swansea. For revenge, Wampanoag warriors set Swansea ablaze and killed eleven men in the town. This was the start of the three-year battle between New England colonists and Indians which is known as King Philip's War.

Both sides slaughtered their enemies and set towns afire. Several more Massachusetts towns, including Springfield, Hadley, and Northampton, were burned by Indians, and hundreds of English colonists were killed. The English lashed back at all Indians, including the "praying Indians," four

69

Indians attacked and burned Brookfield.

thousand of whom were forced into a prison camp.

Although the colonists outnumbered the Indians in New England 60,000 to 35,000, for six months it appeared that the Indians would win King Philip's War. In outlying areas frightened colonists left their homes for the safety of Boston and the other larger towns. The Indians were winning back the frontier, just as Metacomet had hoped.

In the end, though, the larger numbers and better weapons of the colonists helped them win. In December of 1675 an army of men from the Plymouth Colony, the Massachusetts Bay Colony, and Connecticut marched to southern Rhode Island, where two thousand Indian men, women, and children were spending the winter in a swampy area. The colonial soldiers set fire to the wigwams and then butchered the Indians as they ran outside. About a thousand Indians died in this Great Swamp Fight which ended the Indians' chances for victory.

Puritan family defends its home during an Indian attack.

Although Metacomet escaped the massacre, he was tracked down in the summer of 1676 and killed. For Massachusetts and the rest of southern New England the war was over by 1676. However, fighting continued in Maine and New Hampshire for two more years. It was estimated that a thousand colonists and several thousand Indians had been killed in King Philip's War.

Many of the surviving Indians fled to New York and Canada to escape the vengeful colonists. Others, including Metacomet's wife and children, were sold as slaves to the West Indies. The colonists celebrated the departure of the Indians. They could now build farms and towns throughout New England on what had once been the Indians' land.

The lure of land attracted more colonists to Massachusetts. By the late 1600s the Plymouth Colony, which occupied southeastern Massachusetts, was home to nearly 10,000 people. The Massachusetts Bay Colony, which was fanning out throughout much of the rest of Massachusetts, was home to about 100,000 colonists.*

* For more information about the Massachusetts Bay Colony see pages 175, 176, and 177

ANNE BRADSTREET (1613?-1672)

Born in the Northamptonshire region of central England, Anne Bradstreet was better educated than nearly all the other English girls of her time. At the age of seven the young Puritan girl found "much comfort in reading the Scriptures," as she later explained, and also enjoyed reading poetry. At about the age of sixteen Anne was married. Soon after, in 1630, she came to live in the Massachusetts Bay Colony with her husband and her parents. Anne and her husband lived in several towns in eastern Massachusetts, including Ipswich and Andover.

By the age of nineteen Anne Bradstreet was creating poems with such titles as "Upon a Fit of Sickness." She continued to write poetry while raising eight children and managing the household for her husband, Simon Bradstreet, who twice was governor of the Massachusetts Bay Colony. Many of Anne Bradstreet's poems were concerned with topics that were so dear to the Puritans—God, death, heaven, and the importance of living a good and useful life here on earth. She also created some beautiful poems about her family.

In 1650 some of Anne Bradstreet's poems were published in England as a book entitled *The Tenth Muse Lately Sprung Up in America*. Not only was *The Tenth Muse* the first book of poetry written in England's North American colonies, it was also the first important book of poetry ever written by an English woman. Anne Bradstreet continued to write poetry for the rest of her life, and in 1678, six years after her death, a second book of her poems was published.

Today, the language and subject matter of most of Anne Bradstreet's poems seem old-fashioned, which is why they are not often read. A few, including these two, will forever be fresh and lovely:

TO MY DEAR AND LOVING HUSBAND

If ever two were one, then surely we.
If ever man were lov'd by wife, then thee;
If ever wife was happy in a man,
Compare with me ye women if you can.
I prize thy love more than whole Mines of gold,
Or all the riches that the East doth hold.
My love is such that Rivers cannot quench,
Nor aught but love from thee, give recompense.
Thy love is such I can no way repay,
The heavens reward thee manifold I pray.
Then while we live, in love lets so persever,
That when we live no more, we may live ever.

TO MY DEAR CHILDREN

This Book by Any yet unread
I leave for you when I am dead,
That being gone, here you may find
What was your liveing mothers mind.
Make use of what I leave in Love
And God shall blesse you from above.

Colonial iron foundry

Chapter IV

The Two Massachusetts Colonies Become One

"It is a shameful thing that you should mind these folks who are out of their wits!"

Condemned "witch" Martha Carrier, shortly before she was hanged in Salem in 1692

New England coin minted 1652.

From the start, the people of the Plymouth Colony and the Massachusetts Bay Colony had helped each other. During the early days, the people of Plymouth had sold livestock and other farm products to the newcomers at Massachusetts Bay. During King Philip's War, the Massachusetts Bay Colony had supplied troops and guns to help defend the smaller Plymouth Colony. With that war over, the two colonies began to work together against a new enemy—the mother country, England. At the heart of the dispute was the question of whether the two Massachusetts colonies and the other English colonies in America should be allowed to trade with anyone they wanted.

Fishing and shipbuilding were important to the success of the Massachusetts colony.

By the late 1600s the American colonies were producing a great variety of goods. Exports from Massachusetts included iron and iron products, dried codfish and other seafoods, corn and other farm crops, furs and animal skins, cloth and clothes, ships, lumber, shoes, whale products, and candles. Because they wanted the greatest possible profits, the merchants of Massachusetts and the other colonies sold some of their products to the West Indies, Africa, and European countries other than England.

English leaders viewed America as a source of inexpensive goods, and did not want the colonists to sell their products elsewhere. During the middle and late 1600s England passed a series of Navigation Acts. These laws made it difficult for the colonists to trade legally with any country except England.

The colonists wanted to choose their own trading partners for another reason besides money. By the late 1600s quite a few families had lived in America for several generations. Over the years they had carved homes out of the wilderness, fought Indians, and labored to earn a living and raise their families—all with little help from England. Many of these people no longer thought of themselves as English citizens who happened to live in America. Instead, they thought of themselves as Americans, and wanted more freedom from the mother country.

Ax and hammer used in the Plymouth Colony.

Because of this desire for more freedom, and because it would have cost them money, the American colonists ignored the Navigation Acts and continued to choose their own trading partners. When English officials tried to enforce the Navigation Acts, the colonists began smuggling their products out of Boston and other ports.

During the early 1680s the king of England, Charles II, threatened to take away the

King James II

Sir Edmund Andros

Massachusetts Bay Colony charter if the colonists would not obey the Navigation Acts. Massachusetts merchants continued to defy the king and in 1684 Charles II nullified the charter, which meant that the Massachusetts Bay Colony no longer governed itself. It became a royal colony—one under the direct control of the king.

In 1686 England's next king, James II, combined the Massachusetts Bay Colony, the Plymouth Colony, New Hampshire, Rhode Island, Connecticut, New Jersey, and New York into a single province. It was called the Dominion of New England. That same year James II chose a Londoner named Sir Edmund Andros as governor of the Dominion of New England.

Soon after his arrival in New England in December of 1686, Andros took actions which angered New Englanders. He imposed taxes, refused to allow colonial lawmakers to meet, and jailed those who opposed him. When James II was overthrown in 1688, New Englanders used the event as an opportunity to revolt against Andros. In the spring of 1689, Andros and other English officials were arrested in Boston. Andros was packed off to England.

With Andros gone, Massachusetts people set up their own government. However, England would not let Massachusetts go back to its old way of ruling itself. In 1691 England's new rulers, William III and Mary II, returned Massachusetts to royal colony status. At the same time, the Massachusetts Bay Colony was combined with the Plymouth Colony to form the Massachusetts Colony, which had Boston as its capital. Conditions were much better for Massachusetts people than they had been under Andros's rule. The colony was allowed to run many of its own affairs through a legislature elected by the colonists. However, any bill passed by the Massachusetts legislature could be vetoed by the king of England or by the royal governor appointed by the king.

THE
CHARTER
Granted by Their Majesties

King WILLIAM
AND
Queen MARY,
TO THE
INHABITANTS
OF THE
PROVINCE
OF THE
Maffachufetts-Bay
IN
NEW-ENGLAND.

Boston in New England:

Printed by B. Green, Printer to the Honourable the Lieut. GOVERNOUR & COUNCIL, for Benjamin Eliot, and Sold at his Shop near the Town-House in King's Street. 1726.

King William and Queen Mary

The year after the Plymouth and Massachusetts Bay colonies were united, trouble brewed in the Salem area. Early in 1692 several young girls suffered fits in which they claimed they were attacked by some invisible forces. It is now thought that the girls had become hysterical after hearing stories about witchcraft. In Salem in the year 1692, however, most people thought that the girls' seizures were Satan's work. The girls accused three women of bewitching them. This began one of colonial America's most tragic episodes—the Salem Witch-Hunt.

At the time, most Christians believed in witches—people who sold their souls to the devil for riches or magical powers.* Witches supposedly could make crops fail and cause people to die. They were believed to have certain moles and other "devil's marks" on their bodies, and were also thought to reveal their true identities in other people's dreams. Throughout the Middle Ages and on into the 1700s witchcraft panics surged through Europe, resulting in the execution of tens of thousands of "witches." During the seventeenth century the same thing happened on a much smaller scale in the American colonies, with the climax occurring in

* For more information about this belief see page 89

Salem, Massachusetts in the early 1690s.

Soon after the girls named the three women as witches, other people in the Salem area began accusing their neighbors of practicing witchcraft. The accusations became an easy way for people to punish their enemies. All one had to do was point to a mole or describe a weird dream to convince others that someone was a witch!

This dramatic painting of the 1692 witchcraft trial of George Jacobs now hangs in the Essex Institute in Salem.

The governor of the Massachusetts Colony, Sir William Phips, appointed a special court to deal with the suspected witches. The accused had no chance for fair trials in this court. For one thing, they could not have lawyers. For another, if they pleaded innocent, the judges said that the devil was making them lie. The only way the accused could save their lives was to plead guilty and name other witches. The result was a steady stream of accusations.

In the summer of 1692 several hundred people were arrested as suspected witches in and around Salem, which was becoming known as the "Witch City." Out of all those suspected witches, nineteen were hanged. The twentieth victim was an elderly farmer named Giles Corey who refused to plead either guilty or not guilty because he wanted no part in the madness. A large pile of rocks was placed on Corey's chest, crushing him to death.

During late 1692 and early 1693 the mass hysteria became so intense that even well-known ministers and politicians were being called witches. When that happened, Governor Phips, whose own wife had been named as a witch, put an end to the trials. In the spring of 1693 about 150 accused persons who were in jail awaiting

Hundreds of suspected witches were arrested between 1692 and 1693. Twenty were found guilty and executed.

trial were released, ending Salem's witchcraft hysteria.

During the next several years, some of the witch-hunters confessed that they had "acted ignorantly" or been "fooled by Satan" into naming innocent persons. This did not help the twenty people who had been executed, but it did serve as an example to later generations. Today when people are persecuted without evidence or a chance to defend themselves, fair-minded people call it a "witch-hunt."

While the citizens of Salem were calling each other "witches," England was having trouble with its archrival, France, over lands in North America. Each nation controlled part of the continent. The English had their colonies along the east coast of what is now the United States. France controlled Canada, which it called New France.

England and France were both interested in seizing the lands held by the other and also in taking control of lands in what is now the central United States. Between 1689 and 1763 England and France fought four wars for control of North America. Collectively known as the French and Indian Wars, the four were:

King William's War (1689-1697)

Queen Anne's War (1702-1713)

King George's War (1744-1748)

The French and Indian War (1754-1763)

Most Indians hated the English for taking their land and for defeating them in several wars. The French, in contrast, were more interested in trading for furs with the Indians than in turning their hunting grounds into farms and towns. For these reasons most Indians who fought in the French and Indian Wars sided with the French, although some did side with the English.

The sparsely settled frontier towns of Massachusetts were attacked many times during

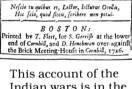

This account of the Indian wars is in the Harvard Library.

Many Indian tribes fought with the French against the English colonists.

the French and Indian Wars. One of the hardest-hit Massachusetts towns was Deerfield, which was attacked and burned by French soldiers and Indians in February of 1704. About fifty of the town's people were killed and more than a hundred were taken captive and marched to Canada. Twenty of the captives were either murdered or died from the cold before reaching Canada.

Thousands of Massachusetts men fought for England during the French and Indian Wars. In 1690 Massachusetts soldiers under the command of Sir William Phips captured Port Royal (now Annapolis Royal) in Nova Scotia, Canada. In 1745 an army of four thousand New England soldiers

French fort at
Louisbourg

organized by Massachusetts Governor William
Shirley sailed up to Nova Scotia's Cape Breton
Island. Led by Massachusetts Chief Justice
William Pepperell, the soldiers seized the French
fortress at the town of Louisbourg on the island.
These efforts helped Great Britain win the French
and Indian Wars.

Despite the battles with the French and the
Indians, Massachusetts continued to grow.
Between 1700 and 1765 the colony's population
rose from not much more than 100,000 to about
250,000. Most of the newcomers came from
England, and by 1765 more than 80 percent of the
population was of English descent. However,
people also came from France, Canada, Scotland,
Ireland, and Germany. There were also several
thousand black Africans in the colony, most of
them slaves.

This variety of people meant that
Massachusetts' days as an almost-exclusively
Puritan colony were over. By the mid-1700s most

Three-penny bill
issued by the
Province of the
Massachusetts Bay in
June, 1722.

Quaker speaker

of those who had been known as Puritans still had the same beliefs. But because they insisted that each separate congregation select its own ministers and control its own affairs, they were now called Congregationalists. Massachusetts was also home to members of the Church of England, as well as Catholics and Quakers.

Not only did Massachusetts people represent various nationalities and religions by the mid-1700s, they also worked at many occupations. The Connecticut River valley and the other fertile regions of Massachusetts attracted tens of thousands of farm families. The coastal towns lured thousands of fishermen to work for the colony's many fishing fleets. Men who wanted to work in the whaling industry came to Nantucket and New Bedford, the two leading whaling ports in the American colonies. Another great attraction of the Massachusetts Colony was the city of Boston, which by 1750 was one of the colonies' leading centers for shipbuilding, fishing, business, and education.

For hundreds of years whaling ships set sail from Massachusetts

COTTON MATHER (1663-1728)

Born in Boston, Massachusetts, Cotton Mather was a descendant of several famous Puritan ministers. His father was Increase Mather, who eventually became president of Harvard College. One of Cotton Mather's grandfathers was Richard Mather, a compiler of *The Bay Psalm Book*. His other grandfather was John Cotton, the most prominent minister of early colonial Massachusetts.

Cotton Mather was so brilliant that by age twelve he had read Cicero and Virgil in Latin and the New Testament in Greek. At twelve he entered Harvard, becoming the youngest student to attend the college up to that time.

Cotton Mather was afraid that his stutter would prevent him from preaching, so after graduating from Harvard at the age of fifteen he turned to the study of medicine. However, he managed to cure himself of the stutter and in early spring of 1680 he became assistant to his father at the Second Church of Boston. During his nearly fifty years as a minister at that church, Cotton Mather earned so great a reputation as a speaker that his sermons were often attended by 1,500 of Boston's approximately 10,000 people.

When he was not in church or preparing a sermon, Cotton Mather studied almost constantly. He taught himself several different languages, and also was an amazingly productive writer. Eventually, Mather wrote more than 450 separate books, including biographies, scientific works, and books on history, philosophy, and religion. His best-known work, *Magnalia Christi Americana*, was the most complete history of New England of the time. Because he wrote books on witchcraft, Cotton Mather has been blamed for helping to create the witchcraft scare in Salem in the early 1690s. However, he did not take part in the witch-hunt, nor did he attend the trials.

Among his other achievements, Cotton Mather helped obtain funds for the new Yale College in Connecticut, and also founded schools for blacks and Indians. He was also one of the first major figures in American medicine. When a smallpox epidemic struck Boston in 1721, he arranged for Dr. Zabdiel Boylston to inoculate people. Nearly all of the approximately 250 people who were so treated remained healthy. For all these accomplishments, Cotton Mather was the most famous person in the American colonies when he died in Boston at the age of sixty-five.

Cotton Mather's book on witchcraft printed in 1689.

BOSTON'S FIRST TOWN-HOUSE
1657~1711

Drawn from the Original
Specifications for
~mas Joy and Bartholomew Bernard
1657

Charles K. Lawrence - 1930

Boston's first
Townhouse drawn
from the original
plans made in 1657.

The TOWN of
BOSTON
IN
New England
by
Capt John Bonner
1722

1722 map of Boston

Chapter V

Life in Colonial Massachusetts in 1750

. . . that Government is the best established, which provides best for the Interest of individuals. The more Good it communicates, the better it is worth defending. . . .

The Boston Gazette, *March 27, 1750*

In the year 1750 Massachusetts was home to more than 200,000 people who lived in more than three hundred towns. Of those towns, Boston, with about 20,000 people, was the largest. Life in Boston had much in common with life in the smaller towns, but it also varied in some important ways.

THE SMALLER TOWNS

Several hundred families lived in the average Massachusetts town in 1750. In the center of a typical town was the community's main church; the school and other public buildings; several businesses, such as a general store and a blacksmith's shop; and a public park, known as the

Old North Church. The lamp that started Paul Revere on his famous ride was hung from the steeple of this church.

Typical New England settlement with the village green in center and buildings surrounded by stockades.

"common" or "green." Most of the townspeople were farmers, and their fields and houses were located throughout the surrounding countryside.

Although some wealthy families owned brick homes, most houses were made of wood. Likewise, although some owned furniture that had been shipped from Europe, most people's beds, tables, and chairs had been fashioned out of New England timber with saw and hammer.

At the center of the home was the fireplace. It kept the house warm during Massachusetts' long winters and on cold nights year-round. Matches had not yet been invented, so the family tried to keep some embers burning even when there was no need for a fire. If the fire went out, a child would take the "fire pan" to a neighbor's house and "borrow some fire," much as children today go to a neighbor to borrow milk or sugar.

The fireplace was also used to cook food. Colonial women cooked stews, vegetables, and soups in a big pot over the fire. Potatoes and eggs were wrapped in wet leaves and then roasted in the fireplace ashes, while meats were placed on a spit and suspended above the fire to cook. Near

Typical New England kitchen

the fireplace there was usually a brick oven in which breads, cakes, beans, potatoes, and pies were baked.

Colonial farm families raised much of their own food. Beans, pumpkins, peas, and corn were popular crops. Cornmeal mush was used to make a dish called hasty pudding, which was eaten so often in some families that children complained it was coming out of their ears. Bean porridge and cooked whole pumpkin were two other popular vegetable dishes.

There were no refrigerators in those days, so a family that slaughtered a cow or a pig (or bagged a deer) shared the meat with neighbors. Then, when the neighbors killed an animal, they also shared it with their neighbors. The colonists also traded food. A family with a milk cow might trade for eggs or for some other food that they wanted.

Cider, made from apples and other fruits, was the most popular drink. It was served with each meal and was drunk instead of water out in the fields. The job of drawing the day's cider from the barrel often fell to the child who awakened last. Although the cider was alcoholic, children drank it, too, because people thought that it spoiled less easily than water. Many Massachusetts children also drank beer as a regular beverage.

Colonial merchant drinking his morning cider

Woman spinning wool

Out in the country most colonial mothers made their families' clothes themselves. They fashioned "Sunday clothes" from fancy European materials purchased in Boston. Everyday clothes were made out of materials at hand. One common material was flax, a plant grown on many Massachusetts farms. The colonial mother used her spinning wheel to spin the flax into linen yarn. The yarn was then woven into cloth on a hand loom, and the cloth was sewn into clothes. As the Indians had done, the colonists also made clothes out of deer and other animal skins.

Colonial women colored the homemade clothes with natural dyes. Brown was made by boiling oak bark, purple came from elderberries and iris petals, orange from sassafras, and crimson from pokeberries. These dyes also were used to color carpets, blankets, and other household items.

One item of dress that was becoming fashionable in 1750 was the wig, which was worn mainly by men and boys. The person's real hair was cut short (to avoid head lice), and then covered by the wig, which was made of goat, horse, or human hair. It is said that Indians who first saw bewigged men thought that they had each grown an extra head. But that may be a colonial tall tale.

In the Massachusetts of 1750 work was strictly divided between men, women, and children. The men built the houses, cleared the fields, and did the heavier farm work. In most cases the men were also the heads of the household, and their word was considered law. Men who owned property were the only ones who could vote. They gathered at large assemblies called town meetings, where they discussed town business

Speaker at a town meeting

and elected unpaid officials called selectmen to govern the town.

The women did the cooking, cleaning, clothes-making, and other household work. The women and children often did the lighter farm work such as seed planting, and women who could handle a gun shot deer and other game that wandered near the farm.

Quite a bit was expected of colonial children. From an early age, girls helped their mothers with the household work, and boys helped their fathers in the fields. Most of the children also went to school, where they concentrated on reading, writing, and penmanship. The most widely used textbook of the time was the *New England Primer*,* which taught the children reading from such rhymes as these:

Homemade candles were used.

A In Adam's Fall
We sinned all.

B Thy Life to mend
This Book attend.

C The Cat doth play
And after slay.

D A Dog will bite
A Thief at Night.

E The Eagle's Flight
Is out of Sight.

F The idle Fool
Is whipt at School.

Most girls learned only to read and write, but many boys went on to study such subjects as

* For more information about the *New England Primer* see page 178

Colonial prayer book

Latin and Greek. Scholarly boys from some of the wealthier families attended Harvard College.

Children as well as adults spent a great deal of time in church. Most Massachusetts colonists spent half of Sunday in church, and the minister's sermon was a major topic of conversation the rest of the week. In addition, during the week there was Lecture Day, when the townspeople went to church to listen to religious talks.

One reason why people thought so much about God and heaven in 1750 was that they did not live very long. Women commonly died of problems during childbirth, and people of all ages died of diseases which today are prevented by vaccines. There were no antibiotics to help those who caught pneumonia, and a person who suffered a compound fracture (one in which the bone sticks through the skin) usually died of infection. The Massachusetts colonists of 1750 lived to an average age of less than forty, as opposed to an average of about seventy-five for Massachusetts residents today.

Boston had a few trained doctors in 1750, but many country towns had none. Because of this, the people used their own remedies, some of which sound strange today. For example, to ease pain during childbirth a woman was supposed to drink cows' milk with ants' eggs and the hair of a young girl mixed into it. A person bitten by a mad dog supposedly could avoid rabies by eating large amounts of onions. The few available doctors prescribed some medicines that were just as outlandish. One Massachusetts doctor of the 1700s said that patients with swollen glands should drink a syrup made of sow bugs in white wine, and that those suffering from trembling should take a bath in liquor mixed with hot human urine! Is it any wonder that the average life span of the colonists was less than forty years?

Because death was an everyday event, and because nearly all of the colonists believed in an afterlife, funerals were not as morbid as some are today. Wealthier families gave gloves and "mourning rings" to the guests as mementoes. The rings were inscribed with such mottoes as "Prepared be To follow me" and "Live to Die."

Although it may sound as if the colonists spent all their time studying, praying, dying, and mourning, they also knew how to have fun. Country people made their work easier by turning

Colonial quilting bee

it into a game. In the autumn, young people held cornhusking bees. A young man who husked an ear of red kernels was allowed to kiss every girl in the circle. A girl who discovered a red ear could give a kiss to her favorite young man. Country women held quilting bees with piles of old shirts and extra pieces of cloth. They traded the fabrics with each other, then sat and visited while they made quilts out of them.

The colonists also enjoyed a variety of sports, games, and entertainments. Boys played football, which was really more like modern soccer. Some individual families were large enough to field an entire football team. Because parents feared that children would not survive, families often had a dozen or more offspring. There were even families with twenty-five or more children in colonial Massachusetts! Other popular sports besides football included horse racing, target shooting with guns, ninepins (bowling), and billiards.

Among the popular family entertainments were Punch and Judy (puppet) shows. From time to time, traveling circus performers came by with such rarely seen animals as elephants and lions, and "flying men" (acrobats) arrived to amaze the townspeople by swinging from ropes off the town's highest steeple.

Of all the special days in the year, the favorite of many Massachusetts people was Thanksgiving, when families gathered for prayer and feasting. Another favorite was Election Day, when candidates passed out "election cakes" and "election beer" to butter up the voters and their families. The colonists were always inventing foods for special occasions. For example, when a woman was about to have a baby, "groaning cakes" and "groaning beer" were served to everyone in the house except the pregnant woman!

LIFE IN BOSTON

With its twenty thousand people, Boston in the year 1750 was the largest and most important city in the thirteen American colonies. The Massachusetts capital was also one of the main cultural and business centers in the thirteen colonies, a leading fishing and shipbuilding city, and an important seaport.

Although Boston in 1750 was not very populous by modern standards, it occupied a much smaller area than it does today and was rather crowded.

View of early Boston

The streets, alleys, and lanes were mostly narrow and winding. Some Boston streets of 1750, including Milk, Beacon, Water, Essex, and Summer, retain those same names today. Others, such as King Street, Queen Street, Cow Lane, Flounder Lane, and Turnagain Alley, have long since undergone name changes.

Some of Boston's main streets were cobbled and had gutters running down the center. The main thoroughfares also had brick sidewalks set off by chains and posts. Most people, however, walked in the middle of the street—except when a carriage came rushing by.

The Boston of 1750 had picture signs in front of the shops, taverns, and other businesses. Although Boston had several fine schools and Harvard College was just across the Charles River in Cambridge, many Bostonians could not read. The pictures on the signs showed the names of the stores. For example, the green dragon in front of one building showed that it was the Green Dragon Tavern. Other stores that could be recognized by their signs included the Chest of Drawers, the Bunch of Grapes, the Red Cross, and the Half Moon.

Green Dragon Tavern sign

This hundred-year-old drawing of Faneuil Hall (center) includes an old store building (at left). Note the date of 1630 shown under the gables of this old building.

Several buildings from 1750 are still Boston landmarks today. Among these are Faneuil Hall, a meeting place and public market just completed in 1742, and the Town House (now known as the Old State House), which was the headquarters of the colonial government. The forty-five-acre public park called Boston Common was also a popular place for strolling, as it still is. But in those days the Common was also used for grazing cattle.

In 1750 as today, one of Boston's busiest sections was its port, at the city's eastern edge. Fishing vessels and passenger and cargo ships constantly came in and out of the harbor. The people of Boston ate many of the same foods, played many of the same games, and raised their families in much the same way as the country people. However, their city's port made it easier

Boston Harbor

Home of a wealthy Boston family. House parties were popular during the colonial period.

for Bostonians to obtain products shipped from Europe. Some Boston merchants made fortunes by shipping products in and out of the port.

The people of the Massachusetts capital in 1750 ranged from being very rich to very poor, much the same as today. Inside their large brick houses, the wealthy lived like kings and queens.

The Old State House in Boston

Most viewed themselves as English rather than Americans, and preferred to import their elegant wigs, clothes, paintings, silverware, furniture, and wines from Europe. The wealthy had servants, and some had slaves,* to see to their every need. The wealthy men were the ones who served as Boston selectmen and as the other town leaders.

Boston also had a large number of what we would call middle-class people who owned shops and worked at various trades. Many of these

* For information about an unusual slave see page 112

107

Bedroom of John Adams

people owned their own homes and had a servant or two. The store owners often had apprentices— young people who were learning a particular trade and who sometimes even lived with them.

Boston was also home to many poor people, who lived crowded together into wooden buildings. They were the ones who suffered the most from malnutrition, disease, and the terrible fires that ravaged the city from time to time.

Included among the city's population in 1750 were several whose names and perhaps even faces would be recognizable today. Fifteen-year-old Paul Revere, thirteen-year-old John Hancock, and twenty-eight-year-old Sam Adams all lived in Boston. Eight miles south of Boston in the town of Braintree (now Quincy) was the home of Sam Adams's fifteen-year-old cousin John Adams, who would one day be the second president of the United States.

Bostonians in 1750 had a choice of several newspapers to read, including *The Boston Weekly News-Letter*, *The Boston Gazette*, and *The Boston Evening Post.*

One topic in the news was the movement of French troops and ships along the coast of Canada. For example, the August 14 *Boston Gazette* reported that:

> *3 Men of War, 2 of 'em of 60 and the other 36 Guns, with 20 Transports, besides a Ship with 300 Women on board, were arrived there [in Louisbourg, Nova Scotia] from France; and that 3 Brigantines with Soldiers, and all Sorts of warlike Stores, and Utensils for building Forts, sailed from Louisbourg about the 20th of July past, and that tho' our Informant could not learn their Destination, they were observed to sail to the Westward—Also, that another Man of War and 20 Transports were soon expected from France.*

Bostonians who read this story on that summer day in 1750 no doubt discussed the likelihood of another war with France. This expectation would prove accurate, because four years later, in 1754, England and France began fighting the last of the French and Indian Wars.

Money was another popular topic in the newspapers of 1750. There was no single system of money in the American colonies at that time. People used money from England, France, and Spain. Individual colonies, including Massachusetts, also printed their own money. However, starting in 1751 Massachusetts and the other New England colonies were going to have to stop issuing their own money, by order of the British Parliament. The Boston newspapers printed articles about the change, and booksellers advertised works that could help people convert their "old tenor" currency into other forms of money.

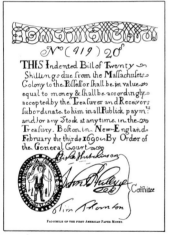

Readers had a choice of many newly published books in 1750. Mysteries and stories on gruesome subjects were popular, as this advertisement from *The Boston Weekly News-Letter* demonstrates:

THIS DAY IS PUBLISHED,
And Sold by F. Draper, in Newbury-Street, Price
Eighteen Pence single, and Twelve Shillings per
Dozen.

An Account of two Inhuman MURDERS, occasion'd
by Jealousy, lately committed at Whittlesey, near
Ely, in England; one by Amy Hutchinson, Aged 17,
who destroyed her Husband by Poison: The other by
John Vicars, who kill'd his Wife by stabbing her
with a Knife as one sticks a Sheep: Both in about
Ten Weeks after Marriage. Chiefly taken from their
own Mouths, of which horrid Facts they were both
convicted, and receiv'd Sentence of Death, October
10th 1749, and were executed November 7th
following: With some Account of their Behaviour.

Political books were also popular, including *Massachusetts in Agony*, which was published in the summer of 1750. A growing mood of political unrest was spreading through the colony. Many people thought that conditions in the Massachusetts Colony would improve if the people had more to say in governing themselves. A few radicals were even hinting that America should become independent of England.

People had to be careful about such talk, however, for the English considered it treasonous. During the next two decades, several events would cause growing numbers of people to think about American independence.

PHILLIS WHEATLEY (1753?-1784)

A baby girl with a name that is now unknown was born in Senegal in western Africa in about 1753. When the girl was around eight years old she was kidnapped and taken in a slave ship to Boston, where she was put up for sale along with a number of other kidnapped blacks. She was bought by a tailor named John Wheatley and his wife, Susannah.

Although slavery was much more common in the South, some northerners also owned slaves. In Massachusetts, a few wealthy people owned slaves right up to and including the time of the Revolution. The slaves in Massachusetts often worked as servants, and this was the job that John and Susannah Wheatley had in mind when they purchased the little black girl in 1761.

Mr. and Mrs. Wheatley named the girl Phillis and trained her to help the several other slaves around their house. Seeing that Phillis was very bright, Mr. and Mrs. Wheatley and their twins, Nathaniel and Mary, taught her to read and write. When Phillis showed that she could understand the most difficult parts of the Bible, the Wheatleys began teaching her Latin, astronomy, geography, history, and literature. By the age of twelve, Phillis was one of the best-educated young ladies—white or black—in all of Boston.

Phillis started writing poetry at about the age of thirteen. She wrote a poem called "On Being Brought From Africa to America," in which she said she was grateful for being introduced to Christianity in the New World. She also wrote "To the University of Cambridge in New England," in which she praised Harvard. Word spread through Boston about the gifted young writer. During the next several years Phillis was often asked to read her poems in people's homes and to write peoms for them for important occasions.

In 1773, when Phillis was about twenty years old, a book of her work was published in London. Called *Poems on Various Subjects, Religious and Moral*, it was the first major poetry volume by a black American. The year that it was published Phillis sailed to London, where she became quite popular.

Phillis was about to meet the king and queen when she was called back to Boston because Mrs. Wheatley was ill. Mrs. Wheatley, Mr. Wheatley, Mary Wheatley, and then Nathaniel Wheatley died in rapid order. Suddenly Phillis, who had been freed by the Wheatley family, was on her own with no way to earn a living.

Phillis Wheatley got married and had three children, but neither she nor her husband could support the family, and two of the children died as babies. Phillis Wheatley spent her last days as a scrubwoman in a Boston boardinghouse, and died penniless at about the age of thirty-one. She left behind several dozen poems, including "A Funeral Poem on the Death of C.E. an Infant of Twelve Months," which has these touching opening lines:

Through airy roads he wings his instant flight
To purer regions of celestial light;
Enlarg'd he sees unnumber'd systems roll,
Beneath him sees the universal whole,
Planets on planets run their destin'd round,
And circling wonders fill the vast profound. . . .

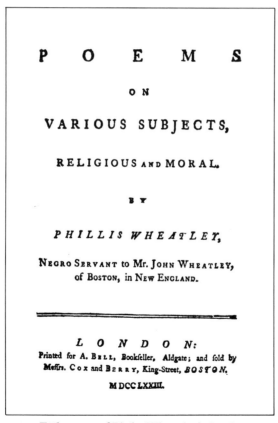

Title page of Philis Wheatley's book

Dramatic painting showing the Americans fighting the British

Chapter VI

"The Shot Heard Round the World:" The Revolution Begins

No people that ever trod the stage of the world have had so glorious a prospect as now rises before the Americans. There is nothing good or great but their wisdom may acquire, and to what heights they will arrive in the progress of time no man can conceive. That Great Britain should continue to insult *and* alienate *the growing millions who inhabit this country . . . is perhaps as glaring an instance of human folly as ever disgraced politicians or put common sense to the blush.*

Sam Adams, writing in The Boston Gazette *in 1773*

Although Great Britain won the French and Indian Wars, the mother country had financial problems when fighting finally ended in 1763. How would Britain repay the debts it had incurred during the wars? Who would pay for the army and navy Britain needed to patrol its newly won American lands? British lawmakers decided that the American colonists should pay a large share of these costs, in the form of taxes.

British tax stamp

James Otis

Great Britain levied many taxes on the American colonists during the 1760s. According to the Stamp Act of 1765, Americans were supposed to buy tax stamps and place them on such legal documents as deeds, diplomas, and licenses. Taxes were also placed on tea, paper, and other items imported from Britain. To keep the colonists from buying these items elsewhere, the British tried to enforce the Navigation Acts, which restricted trade with non-British nations.

Most Americans thought it was unfair for them to bear the mother country's financial burden. During the 1760s the Boston lawyer James Otis (1725-1783) gave speeches in which he said, "Taxation without representation is tyranny!" His words became a catch phrase among the colonists who gathered in meeting halls and taverns to discuss the tax problem. It meant that the colonists hated being taxed by Great Britain while having no representatives in the British lawmaking body called the Parliament.

The American colonists—especially those in Massachusetts—found ways to avoid the taxation. They smuggled goods from non-British countries into Boston and other ports, just as they had done during the early days of the

Navigation Acts of the 1600s. Many colonists also boycotted (refused to buy) goods shipped from England. They made the goods themselves or did without them.

Massachusetts was the center for American unrest during the 1760s. One reason for this was that Boston was a major port, and the British taxes on imported goods cost the city's merchants money. Massachusetts also had the best-educated populace of all the colonies. Educated people were aware of the spirit of rebellion that was sweeping through other nations where people felt oppressed. They were also good at writing letters to British lawmakers and holding meetings at which British injustices were discussed.

Throughout the colonies political groups were formed to deal with what people were calling British oppression. The best-known group in all the colonies was Boston's Sons of Liberty. The

The true Sons of Liberty

And Supporters of the Non-Importation Agreement,

ARE determined to refent any the leaft Infult or Menace offer'd to any one or more of the feveral Committees appointed by the Body at Faneuil-Hall, and chaftife any one or more of them as they deferve ; and will alfo fupport the Printers in any Thing the Committees fhall defire them to print.

☞AS a Warning to any one that fhall affront as aforefaid, upon fure Information given, one of thefe Advertifements will be pofted up at the Door or Dwelling-Houfe of the Offender.

Handbill distributed by the "Sons of Liberty"

Colonists raise a Liberty Pole

Tax stamps were burned publicly in protest.

Sons did not just talk about "freedom," "liberty," and "taxation without representation." They also staged demonstrations and riots to protest British taxes, and sometimes beat up Americans who continued to do business with the British.

The Stamp Act, which required colonists to buy stamps for official documents, enraged the Sons of Liberty. In mid-August of 1765 a mob that included some Sons of Liberty marched into Boston Common. The mob burned a dummy made to look like British Stamp Act official Andrew Oliver. Chanting "Liberty, property, and no stamps!" the mob then smashed a building owned by Oliver. A few days later the Boston mob marched to the home of the Massachusetts Colony's Chief Justice Thomas Hutchinson. To protest Hutchinson's efforts to enforce the Stamp Act, the mob smashed and burned his home.

Samuel Adams

The leader of the Massachusetts radicals was a middle-aged Bostonian named Samuel Adams.* By 1765 the forty-three-year-old Adams had failed at every job he had tried and was deeply in debt. The main reason for this was that he spent nearly all of his time combating British injustice. He regularly wrote essays on the Stamp Act and other political issues for Boston newspapers. He stayed up late writing letters on the same topics to British officials and to Americans throughout the colonies. Sam Adams never took part in the Sons of Liberty's violent acts. But he had named and helped to organize the group, and he is thought to have secretly directed its activities.

In fall of 1765, at about the time that he was elected to the Massachusetts colonial legislature,

* For more information about Samuel Adams see page 142

Sam Adams helped to organize the Stamp Act Congress. In October of 1765 representatives from Massachusetts and eight other colonies gathered in New York City to attend the congress. This was one of the first times that representatives from many colonies gathered together to work on a common cause.

Americans protested so strongly against the Stamp Act that the British Parliament repealed it in 1766. When news of that reached Boston, the well-known merchant John Hancock* placed a huge barrel of wine out on the Common so that Bostonians could celebrate. Hancock also put on a fireworks display near where the Massachusetts State House now stands.

Americans continued to riot and demonstrate against the remaining tax laws. One defiant act which became famous throughout the colonies occurred in 1768, when the *Liberty*, one of John Hancock's ships, arrived in Boston with a cargo of wine. A British tax officer came to inspect the imported wine, but the crew locked him in a cabin. Because defiant acts like this were happening regularly in Boston, in the fall of 1768 Britain sent troops into the city to try to keep order.

John Hancock

* For more information about John Hancock see page 143

British troops were sent to Boston to keep order.

To Sam Adams, the arrival of British troops was a golden opportunity to stir up anti-British feeling. Adams founded *Journal of Events*, a newspaper that described crimes supposedly committed by the British soldiers in Boston. Actually, Sam Adams made up most of the stories, but he saw nothing wrong with lying for a good cause!

Most of the colonists during the 1760s merely wanted better treatment from Great Britain. But a handful of them—including Sam Adams of Massachusetts and Patrick Henry of Virginia—viewed the cause differently. They wanted the American colonies to become independent of Great Britain. By the late 1760s, Sam Adams was the leading spokesman in all the colonies for those desiring American independence.

While Sam Adams was using his pen to protest the presence of the British soldiers, other Bostonians were more violent. Gangs ran past the soldiers yelling "bloody-backs" and "lobster-backs" (because of their red uniforms), and also pelted them with snowballs and rocks. The well-trained British soldiers ignored this kind of behavior—until one day in spring of 1770.

On March 5, 1770, a group of Bostonians began throwing stones and taunting a group of British soldiers on guard on King Street (now State Street). To avoid trouble, the British officer ordered his men back to their barracks. The crowd then turned to the British sentry at the

Boston Massacre

State House and hurled objects at him while threatening to kill him. British soldiers rushed out to help the man, but the crowd began daring them to fire their guns. Thinking that the order to shoot had really been given, the confused soldiers fired into the crowd. Five persons were killed, including Crispus Attucks (1723?-1770), who is thought to have been a runaway slave. Half a dozen others were wounded.

Crispus Attucks

Handbill listing those who were killed or wounded in what the revolutionary forces called the Boston Massacre.

The King Street incident was really just a street brawl, but Sam Adams wrote articles in which he called it the "Boston Massacre." Soon people throughout the colonies were complaining about the cruel British soldiers who had fired into a crowd of innocent Bostonians. The Boston Massacre, as it is still called today, put the colonists into a fighting mood.

Meanwhile, British lawmakers across the ocean wanted to show that they were still in charge of their American colonies. In 1770 Parliament repealed most of the taxes on goods brought into the American colonies. However, it kept the tax on tea to show that it still had the right to levy such taxes. Then in 1773 Parliament passed the Tea Act, which lowered the price of tea while maintaining the tax on the beverage. The purpose of the Tea Act was to lure Americans back to drinking English tea and to coax them into paying the taxes.

When a large shipment of tea arrived in Boston Harbor aboard three British ships, Bostonians held town meetings to discuss what to do. They decided to ask Thomas Hutchinson, who was now royal governor, to return the tea to England. When Hutchinson refused to do this, Sam Adams and

After the massacre, Sam Adams demanded that Governor Hutchinson withdraw the British soldiers from Boston.

some other Bostonians decided to turn Boston Harbor into a "teapot," as they put it.

On December 16, 1773, about seven thousand Bostonians attended a town meeting at the Old South Church to decide the next course of action. During the meeting Sam Adams suddenly rose and said: "This meeting can do nothing more to save the country!" Evidently these words were a

signal to a group of about fifty men who were dressed as Indians and waiting outside the church. The moment Adams finished talking the men ran down to the wharf, boarded the three ships, and dumped all 340 chests of tea into Boston Harbor.

Many Americans applauded the Boston Tea Party, as it was called. In a letter, John Adams* (who was Sam Adams's cousin) called it "the grandest event which has yet happened since the controversy with Britain opened." To the British however, the Tea Party showed that Bostonians no longer respected law and order. To punish them, Great Britain ordered the port of Boston closed until the destroyed tea was paid for.

John Adams

Bostonians held another town meeting. Although thousands of them were put out of work by the port closing, they decided not to pay the British tea company for its lost goods. In fact, the closing of the port not only put many Massachusetts people into a warlike mood, it also helped unite Americans throughout the colonies.

Down in Virginia, members of the House of Burgesses took Thomas Jefferson's suggestion and spent June 1, 1774, the day Boston's port was first closed, in prayer and fasting to show their

Opposite page:
Painting of the
Boston Tea Party

* For more information about John Adams see page 144

support for the Massachusetts patriots. When people in Connecticut, New York, and Rhode Island heard that Boston's laborers, sailors, and merchants were suffering due to the closing, they sent corn, beef, fish, and sugar to the city. Carolina colonists sent rice, and some in Maryland provided bread. Salem and Marblehead, towns near Boston, allowed Boston merchants to share their ports.

The Boston Tea Party inspired several other similar affairs. In April of 1774, New York City patriots dumped a shipment of tea into the harbor, and in October patriots in Annapolis, Maryland burned the British ship *Peggy Stewart* with its tea cargo. In December of 1774, New Jersey colonists dressed as Indians burned some British tea in an incident known as the Greenwich Tea Burning. Also in December of 1774 the Boston silversmith Paul Revere,* who later was to make a much more famous ride, traveled to New Hampshire to warn patriots there of a British military buildup in the area. In one of the first American military acts against the British, colonists at New Castle, New Hampshire seized gunpowder and other supplies from a British fort on the night of December 15, 1774.

* For more information about Paul Revere see page 142

Paul Revere & Son,
BELL and CANNON FOUNDERY, at the
North Part of BOSTON

Paul Revere (left) was a silversmith.
He also owned an iron foundry and
used the logo (above) as his
business sign.

From their earliest days, towns in
Massachusetts and in the other American
colonies had maintained militia (emergency
military forces) in case of attack by Indians or
foreign armies. Because of all the trouble with
Britain, during the 1770s the colonial militia
readied themselves for battle. In Massachusetts
some of the militia were called minutemen
because they could prepare for battle at a
minute's notice. Other colonies also had
minutemen, but the best-known ones were from
Massachusetts.

Sam Adams, who by now was considered by
British officials to be "the most dangerous man in
Massachusetts," realized that people in the
thirteen colonies would have to work together if it

came down to a fight with England. In the summer of 1773 Sam Adams suggested a meeting of representatives from all the colonies. Benjamin Franklin suggested the same thing at about the same time, which is why historians do not agree as to which man should be given credit for the idea.

American leaders throughout the colonies organized a convention, called the First Continental Congress. It opened in Philadelphia on September 5, 1774. Georgia sent no delegates, but agreed to support the Congress's decisions. The other twelve colonies sent a total of fifty-six delegates. The Massachusetts Colony sent Sam Adams, his cousin John Adams, and also Thomas Cushing and Robert Treat Paine.

When the First Continential Congress opened, most Americans still thought that better treatment from Britain could be gained peacefully. There was a general feeling—held by many representatives at the Continental Congress—that the Massachusetts leaders were too warlike toward Britain. Nonetheless, Congress agreed that Massachusetts should prepare itself in case the colony was attacked by British troops. Congress also agreed on some complaints

Robert Treat Paine

Patrick Henry delivers his "Give me liberty or give me death" speech in Richmond, Virginia on March 23, 1775.

regarding taxes and other matters which it presented to Great Britain. The First Continental Congress closed in late October of 1774. Delegates agreed to meet again in May of 1775 if Great Britain refused their requests.

When Britain would not give in, Patrick Henry of Virginia said in his famous "Give me liberty or give me death" speech that "the next gale that sweeps from the north will bring to our ears the clash of resounding arms!" He was predicting that war with Britain would soon begin somewhere north of Virginia. Most people thought that if it came to war, it would begin in Massachusetts, the colony that had feuded so bitterly with Great Britain.

In April of 1775 the British General Thomas Gage, who had replaced Thomas Hutchinson as Massachusetts royal governor and who was also in charge of British forces in America, learned two pieces of news from his spies. The first was that the colonists had gathered a large supply of gunpowder in Concord, Massachusetts, about twenty miles northwest of Boston. Second, Gage learned that two important rebel leaders, Sam Adams and John Hancock, were staying at a house in Lexington, Massachusetts, several miles from Concord. Sam Adams and Hancock were on the list of Americans to be executed if captured. Gage believed that getting rid of them would put an end to much of the trouble in America.

On the night of April 18, 1775, General Gage led British troops secretly out of Boston. Their goals were to capture Sam Adams and Hancock in Lexington and then seize the gunpowder in Concord. Luckily for the patriots, a young American boy who had been hired by British officers to watch their horses outside a tavern

General Thomas Gage

Paul Revere warns a minuteman that the British troops were marching to Lexington and Concord.

heard them discussing the plan. The boy told the landlord of Boston's Green Dragon Tavern, where the Sons of Liberty and other patriots met. Word was sent to Paul Revere, messenger for the Boston patriots, that the British were heading for Lexington and Concord.

Revere set out on his famous ride at about ten o'clock that night. On the way, he stopped at nearly every farmhouse he passed to warn people that the British were coming. Near midnight, Revere arrived at the house in Lexington where Sam Adams and John Hancock were staying. A guard at the house refused to let Revere inside, saying that he was making too much noise.

"Noise!" yelled Revere. "You'll have noise enough before long. The Regulars [British soldiers] are coming out!"

Finally, Revere was allowed to warn Sam Adams and John Hancock of the British approach. Revere and two other riders, William Dawes and Dr. Samuel Prescott, then set out for Concord. Paul Revere was captured by the British (and soon released without his horse) and Dawes was injured while fleeing a British patrol, but Dr. Prescott made it to Concord.

The Concord patriots immediately hid their gunpowder and weapons. Meanwhile, five miles away in Lexington, Sam Adams and John Hancock made their way out of town as church bells roused the minutemen from their beds. By one o'clock in the morning of April 19, 1775,

The minutemen prepare for battle.

about 130 minutemen had gathered on Lexington Green. The men waited for one hour, then another. When the British did not appear, they disbanded with the understanding that they should return the moment the British were spotted.

At dawn a lookout breathlessly rode into Lexington. "The lobsterbacks are down the road!" he yelled. By the time the British appeared, just half of Lexington's 150 minutemen had arrived on the Green.

Those approximately seventy-five men standing on Lexington Green were a shabby group. They had no uniforms. They carried various kinds of guns instead of a standard weapon. Some of them were grandfathers, and others were teenaged boys.

Some historians dispute it, but according to tradition Captain John Parker (1729-1775),* leader of the Lexington minutemen, gave his men a now-famous speech as the British appeared. "Stand your ground," he is supposed to have said. "Don't fire unless fired upon. But if they mean to have a war, let it begin here!"

The leader of the British advance party was Major John Pitcairn. Pitcairn studied the ragtag

* For John Parker's description of Lexington see page 180

Major Pitcairn's pistols

bunch of farmers who had assembled against the well-armed British redcoats. "Disperse ye rebels, ye villains, disperse, disperse in the name of the king!" Pitcairn ordered. "Lay down your arms."

Because they were so badly outnumbered, the Americans began to head for home. The next second someone fired a shot—whether from the British or American side is still debated. Suddenly the British began mowing down the nearly helpless minutemen, only a few of whom managed to return the fire.

Eight colonists were killed in the brief battle fought at Lexington at dawn on April 19, 1775. One of the eight, Jonathan Harrington, managed to crawl from the Green to the doorstep of his home, where he died in front of his wife and son. Ten Americans as well as one British soldier were wounded in the Battle of Lexington, which began the revolutionary war.

"Cease firing, cease firing!" shouted British Major John Pitcairn, who had lost control of his men. The British yelled out three cheers for their victory. Then they set out for nearby Concord, where, with other British troops, they expected to make equally quick work of any opposition.

Battle of Lexington drawn by Hammatt Billings.

Once in Concord, the British destroyed whatever gunpowder and weapons they found. They also burned the town hall and the "Liberty Pole" where Concord people gathered for patriotic meetings.

Meanwhile, news of the massacre in Lexington had spread, and hundreds of minutemen from around the countryside were making their way to

Concord. By 9:30 A.M. about four hundred very angry Americans had gathered near the North Bridge, outside Concord. As smoke rose from the town's burning buildings, Colonel James Barrett, commander of the Concord minutemen, spoke with the other leaders. A farmer named Joseph Hosmer is said to have asked Barrett, "Will you let them burn the town down?" The American leaders decided to attack the hundred or so redcoats who were guarding the bridge, then march into Concord and drive the main body of British troops out of the town.

When they saw the minutemen marching toward them, the British fired warning shots into the water. This time the Americans did not scatter. Nor did they back off when the redcoats fired their muskets at them, killing two men and wounding several others. "For God's sake, fire!" yelled an American officer. Suddenly hundreds of Americans were shooting at the British, who lost several officers in the very first volley. Because the battle at the bridge near Concord marked the first time that the Americans made a major attack on the British, the writer Ralph Waldo Emerson later called it "the shot heard round the world."

Flag carried by the Bedford Militia Company at Concord Bridge. According to William S. Appleton of Massachusetts, "It was originally designed in England in 1660-70 for the three-county troops of Middlesex, and became one of the accepted standards of the organized Militia of the State, and as such it was used by the Bedford Company."

The British retreat from Concord

With the Americans in hot pursuit, the stunned British soldiers retreated across the bridge to the main body of redcoats in Concord. Although they were better armed, the British were outnumbered by about 1,500 to 700. The Americans had another advantage. The British had been trained to fight out in the open. The Americans had learned from the Indians that it was wiser to fight from concealed places. The Americans hid behind trees, stone walls, and farm buildings. As the British left Concord and headed back to Boston, the Americans sniped at them from their hiding places. Soon the British were falling like targets in a shooting contest as they ran for their lives.

In places, the British managed to fight back. Near Medford an American patriot named Samuel Whittemore was crouching behind a stone wall near a tavern when some British soldiers passed. The eighty-year-old Whittemore shot one of them dead and wounded another before the British noticed him and shot him in the face. The enraged British soldiers stabbed Whittemore thirteen times with their bayonets. Amazingly, Samuel Whittemore survived and lived to the age of ninety-eight. There was also fighting inside houses and taverns as some of the British tried to find the hiding places of the American marksmen.

Fortunately for the British, reinforcements under the command of General Hugh, Lord Percy, met them during their dash to Boston. If not for that, nearly all seven hundred of them might have been killed. As it was, when the British finally entered Boston they found that nearly three hundred of their soldiers had been killed or

Lord Percy

wounded in the running Battle of Concord. The Americans lost about a hundred in the battle.

As the world's most powerful nation, Great Britain had thought of the American rebels as little more than a swarm of pests. The battle at Concord had proven otherwise. Lord Percy, the general who had helped the redcoats avoid a total massacre at Concord, informed the English people of this when he said:

> *Whoever looks upon them [the American troops] as an irregular mob will find himself much mistaken. They have men amongst them who know very well what they are about. . . . The rebels . . . are determined to go through with it [a war].*

Statue of a minuteman in Lexington

Just as many Americans had expected, the "clash of resounding arms" had begun in Massachusetts. The colonists had fought bravely on that first day of the war. At the Battle of Concord, they also had displayed good discipline and organization. Yet in those first days of fighting few people thought that the colonists had a chance to win the revolutionary war.

Monument at Lexington

SAMUEL ADAMS (1722-1803)

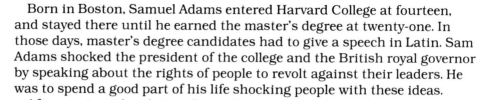

Born in Boston, Samuel Adams entered Harvard College at fourteen, and stayed there until he earned the master's degree at twenty-one. In those days, master's degree candidates had to give a speech in Latin. Sam Adams shocked the president of the college and the British royal governor by speaking about the rights of people to revolt against their leaders. He was to spend a good part of his life shocking people with these ideas.

After receiving his degree, Sam Adams entered the working world, but failed at everything he tried. He was fired from his bank job because he spent too much time talking politics in taverns when he was supposed to be working. A business he started failed, partly because he made a large loan to a poverty-stricken friend. At the age of thirty-four Adams finally landed a good job as Boston's tax collector, but he felt so sorry for those who owed money that he flopped at this, too. In order to survive, Adams and his two wives (the first died young) and children had to depend on gifts of food and clothes from friends.

One reason why Sam Adams was such a bad businessman was that he spent most of his time and energy on the American cause. Earlier than any other well-known American, he came out in favor of American independence, which became the goal of his life. Adams organized political meetings, wrote letters and newspaper articles, and is believed to have planned the Boston Tea Party. So dedicated was Sam Adams to the cause that he became known as "the Chief of the Revolution" and the "Father of American Independence."

Although no one except George Washington did as much as Sam Adams to help establish the United States, he is not as famous as many other patriots. One reason for this was his dislike of the spotlight. He preferred to plan strategy and let others receive the glory.

At the end of the revolutionary war Sam Adams returned to Boston, where he lived once more in what he called "honorable poverty." He also served as governor of the state of Massachusetts from 1793 to 1797.

PAUL REVERE (1735-1818)

Born in Boston, Paul Revere attended school until the age of thirteen when he went to work for his father, a well-known silversmith. By the time his father died five years later, Paul was so good at making silver bowls and spoons that he was able to take charge of the silversmith shop himself.

Paul Revere was married twice (his first wife died young, as was so common) and eventually became the father of sixteen children. The silversmith shop did not bring in enough money for his large family, so to add to his income Paul Revere shod horses, designed picture frames, and even went into the business of making false teeth.

In his spare time Revere attended political meetings, and during the 1760s became friends with Sam Adams and John Hancock. Paul Revere helped the American cause by creating engravings and political cartoons that made fun of the British rulers, and in 1773 he was one of the "Indians" at the Boston Tea Party.

Because he was dependable and a good rider, Paul Revere became the chief messenger for the Massachusetts patriots. He carried news of the Boston Tea Party to New York City, and when the British closed the port of Boston he made a round-trip ride of more than seven hundred miles to tell the people of New York and Philadelphia about it. Of course Paul Revere's most famous ride was the one he made to Lexington on the night of April 18, 1775, when he warned Samuel Adams and John Hancock that the British were coming.

During the revolutionary war Paul Revere commanded a fort at Castle Island in Boston Harbor. He also made cannons for the Continental army, designed and printed the first United States paper money, and engraved the Massachusetts state seal, which is still used today.

After the war ended, Paul Revere returned to his silver business in Boston. He became so fine a craftsman that his pieces are highly regarded today. He also made several hundred church bells, many of which are still rung in New England churches. Paul Revere, who wore his revolutionary war uniform every day for the rest of his life, lived until the age of eighty-three.

JOHN HANCOCK (1737-1793)

Born in Braintree, Massachusetts, John Hancock was the son of a poor minister. When John was seven years old his father died, and the boy was sent to live with his uncle, the wealthy Boston merchant Thomas Hancock. After graduating from Harvard at seventeen, John went to work in his Uncle Thomas's business. When Thomas Hancock died in 1764 and left him seventy thousand pounds, twenty-seven-year-old John Hancock instantly became the wealthiest man in all of New England.

During the 1760s John Hancock added his voice to the growing number of Americans who were bitter about the British taxes. In 1768 he became a hero to the American patriots when the crew of his ship, the *Liberty*, locked a British tax agent in a cabin. Because Hancock gave so much money to the American cause, people joked that "Sam Adams writes the letters [to the newspapers] and John Hancock pays the postage."

In April of 1775, John Hancock was in Lexington with Sam Adams as the British approached. When Paul Revere warned them that the British were coming, Hancock took out his gun and sword and was about to go out with the minutemen to defend Lexington. Adams had to persuade Hancock that he was too valuable to be killed in the war's first skirmish.

After leaving Lexington, Hancock and Adams made their way to Philadelphia, where they served in the Second Continental Congress. Hancock was elected president of the Congress, and as such he was the first person to sign the Declaration of Independence. People still speak of writing their "John Hancock" when they sign important papers.

After the revolutionary war was won, John Hancock was more popular than ever in Massachusetts. He was elected the state's first governor by a huge margin, and was serving his ninth term as governor when he died.

JOHN ADAMS (1735-1826)

Born in Braintree (today Quincy), John Adams attended Harvard, as so many prominent young Massachusetts men did in those days. After graduating in 1755, he taught school at Worcester for a year and then took up the study of law.

In 1768, the year that he moved with his wife and children to Boston, John Adams successfully defended John Hancock from a smuggling charge. Then in 1770 he successfully defended the British soldiers who had taken part in the Boston Massacre. Because the people of Massachusetts realized that Adams had acted fairly, his reputation grew even though he had taken the side of British soldiers.

John Adams gradually became convinced that the colonies must separate from Great Britain, and that he had to take an active role in the process. Adams was selected as a delegate from Massachusetts to the two Continental Congresses. At the Second Congress he was instrumental in the selection of George Washington as commander in chief of the Continental army. He also served on the committee that drafted the Declaration of Independence.

Early in 1778 the Continental Congress decided that John Adams should go to Paris to help obtain French aid for the American cause. John and Abigail Adams decided that their son, John Quincy Adams, would benefit by spending some time in France. John Adams and his son boarded the *Boston* and were several days out of Massachusetts when the ship began to battle with a British vessel. John grabbed his musket and went out onto the deck with John Quincy. Suddenly a cannonball thudded into the *Boston* near where father and son were standing. Had the cannonball struck a few feet away, it could have caused the deaths of two men destined to become United States presidents—John and John Quincy Adams.

After the Revolution, John Adams helped negotiate the peace treaty with Great Britain. He served his country in many ways for the rest of his life. He was the first United States minister to Great Britain. In the election for first president of the United States in 1789, George Washington gathered the most votes. John Adams came in second. According to the rules of the time, George Washington became the first president and John Adams became the first vice-president.

In 1796 John Adams was elected second president of the United States, and he served as president until 1801. John Adams died at the age of nearly ninety-one on July 4, 1826—exactly fifty years to the day after the adoption of America's Declaration of Independence.

Family takes up arms to fight for America's independence from British rule.

Chapter VII

A Nation Is Born

July 21, 1776 Boston
Last Thursday after hearing a very good Sermon I
went with the Multitude into Kings Street [in Boston]
to hear the proclamation for independence
[Declaration of Independence] read and
proclaimed. . . . When Col. Crafts read from the
Belcona [balcony] of the State House the
Proclamation, great attention was given to every
word. As soon as he ended, the cry from the Belcona,
was God save our American States and then 3
cheers . . . rended the air, the Bells rang, the
privateers fired . . . the cannon were discharged . . .
and every face appeard joyfull. . . .

From a letter written by Abigail Adams to
her husband, John Adams

Many people think that, following the Lexington
and Concord battles, Americans were 100 percent
in favor of fighting Britain. This was not the case.
In fact, in spring of 1775 about one fourth of the
colonists sided with Britain. These people—
mostly wealthy individuals who did business with
Britain—were called Tories, or Loyalists. Even
most of those who took the American side hoped
that, despite what had happened at Lexington

A Tory merchant, loyal to the king of England, is heckled by the townspeople.

and Concord, things still could be settled peacefully.

On May 10, 1775, just three weeks after the Lexington and Concord battles, the Second Continental Congress opened in Philadelphia. John Hancock of Massachusetts was elected president of the Congress, a position he held until 1777. Sam Adams (who along with Ben Franklin was one of the two most renowned men at the Congress) tried to convince the delegates that America should separate from Great Britain. Most of the delegates wanted the colonies to have more freedom from Britain but were against complete American independence.

Nevertheless, Congress realized that the colonies must be prepared in case war continued. One of Congress's first tasks was to select a commander for the American troops. John Adams nominated the leading military man in the colonies, George Washington of Virginia, as commander-in-chief of the Continental army. Sam Adams seconded the motion, and Washington was elected unanimously.

Massachusetts treasury note

Meanwhile, Britain had decided to crush the rebellion rather than give in to the colonists' demands. In June of 1775 it appeared that the British and the Americans were headed toward a tremendous battle, again in Massachusetts. The British controlled Boston, but the Americans held the surrounding countryside. Day after day, colonial soldiers from Massachusetts, New Hampshire, Connecticut, Rhode Island, Pennsylvania, and other colonies poured into the Boston area. By mid-June the colonists had sixteen thousand men near Boston and felt ready to strike.

The American leaders learned that the British planned to fortify the hills in Charlestown (now a section of Boston), north of the Charles River. In order to beat them to it, Colonel William Prescott

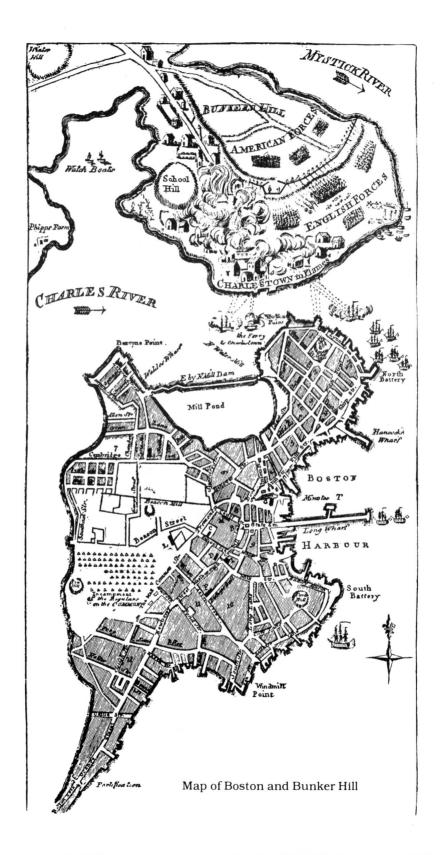

Map of Boston and Bunker Hill

BOSTON

CHARLES TO

Dramatic engraving showing the British attack on Charlestown and the American rebels.

of Groton, Massachusetts was ordered to take a thousand men and fortify Bunker Hill in Charlestown. On the night of June 16, 1775, Prescott led his men to Bunker Hill, but instead decided to fortify nearby Breed's Hill, which was closer to the heart of Boston.

All night the Americans worked on their hilltop fortifications. Early the next morning when the British in Boston discovered that the Americans were nearby at Breed's Hill, General William Howe led 2,500 redcoats across the Charles River to attack them.

As the British advanced, William Prescott is said to have told the colonists: "Men, you are all marksmen—don't one of you fire until you see the whites of their eyes."

Unfortunately for them, the British did not yet realize that it was better to fight from a hiding place than out in the open. Expecting to drive the Americans away fairly easily, the British soldiers marched up Breed's Hill. When they came within fifty feet of the colonists, the Americans fired. The British had to retreat, leaving hundreds of bleeding soldiers behind. A second time the British assaulted the hill, with the same result. The Americans were outnumbered and were running out of powder, however. They had to retreat from the third charge.

British troops march into battle accompanied by drummers.

The people of Boston sat on their roofs and watched the battle between the Americans and the British.

The Battle of Bunker Hill (which really was fought at Breed's Hill) was one of the bloodiest battles of the entire revolutionary war. Because the British took the hill, they were credited with winning the battle. But in terms of casualties, the British had lost. More than one thousand of their troops had been killed or wounded, while the Americans had suffered about four hundred casualties. On that one day, June 17, 1775, more British officers were killed than in the rest of the war. "Another such victory and we'll lose the war!" people in England told each other about this battle. Americans bragged that "We have more ground to sell them at the same price!"

George Washington arrived in Massachusetts shortly after the Battle of Bunker Hill and spent

George Washington is greeted by the people of Cambridge.

several months training the troops. When spring of 1776 came, Washington led his troops to Dorchester Heights, overlooking Boston. Realizing that Washington's cannons were aimed at them from above, the British fled Boston on Saint Patrick's Day, March 17, 1776. It should be remembered that the Americans who had fought so well at the Battle of Bunker Hill had paved the way for Washington to take Boston.

Medal struck by Congress in honor of the recapture of Boston.

In Philadelphia, meanwhile, the Second Continental Congress was still debating what to do. As 1776 wore on, more and more members of Congress decided that America should declare its independence. There were several reasons for this. For one, it was clear that full-scale war was already underway. Second, each day more Americans throughout the thirteen colonies were coming out in favor of separation from England. The work of Sam and John Adams during this period was also vital. The Adams cousins spoke for hours with undecided members of Congress to swing them to the side of independence.

In June of 1776 Congress appointed a committee to create a declaration of independence. This did not mean that Congress favored separation from Great Britain. That

question would be settled later by a vote. The purpose of writing the declaration was to have it ready in case Congress decided that America should be independent.

Five men were assigned to the declaration committee. They were John Adams of Massachusetts, Benjamin Franklin of Pennsylvania, Robert R. Livingston of New York, Roger Sherman of Connecticut, and Thomas Jefferson of Virginia.

Sherman and Livingston could not write well enough, and Ben Franklin was too sick to draft the declaration. That left it up to two future United States presidents—John Adams of Massachusetts and Thomas Jefferson of Virginia—to do it. Years later, John Adams described the talk he had with Jefferson about which one of them should draft the declaration:

Thomas Jefferson: "You should do it!"

John Adams: "Oh! No."

TJ: "Why will you not? You ought to do it."

JA: "I will not."

TJ: "Why?"

JA: "Reasons enough."

TJ: "What can be your reasons?"

JA: "Reason first—you are a Virginian, and a Virginian ought to appear at the head of this business. Reason second—I am obnoxious, suspected, and unpopular. You are very much otherwise. Reason third—you can write ten times better than I can."

TJ: "Well, if you are decided, I will do as well as I can."

John Adams said that "a Virginian ought to appear at the head of this business" because some people still considered the Revolution to be Massachusetts' war. The American leaders wanted to involve people from other colonies in revolutionary affairs so that Americans would see it as a nationwide struggle. There were political reasons behind the choice of other important colonial officials, too. For example, one reason for George Washington's selection as commander in chief of the Continental army was that it would help involve Virginia and the other southern colonies. The fact that John Hancock was New England's richest man helped him be elected president of the Continental Congress. The colonial leaders wanted to show the world that at least one wealthy person sided with the Americans.

Thomas Jefferson wrote the Declaration of Independence during two weeks of late June, 1776. When he finished it, Jefferson showed the Declaration to the other men on the committee. They suggested just a few small changes.

On July 2, 1776, Congress was ready to vote on the independence issue. By this time everyone could see that at least nine of the colonies were in favor of independence. That was more than the two thirds majority needed to pass a resolution. When the vote came, some who voted for independence really wanted the colonies to remain part of Great Britain. They voted for

Thomas Jefferson

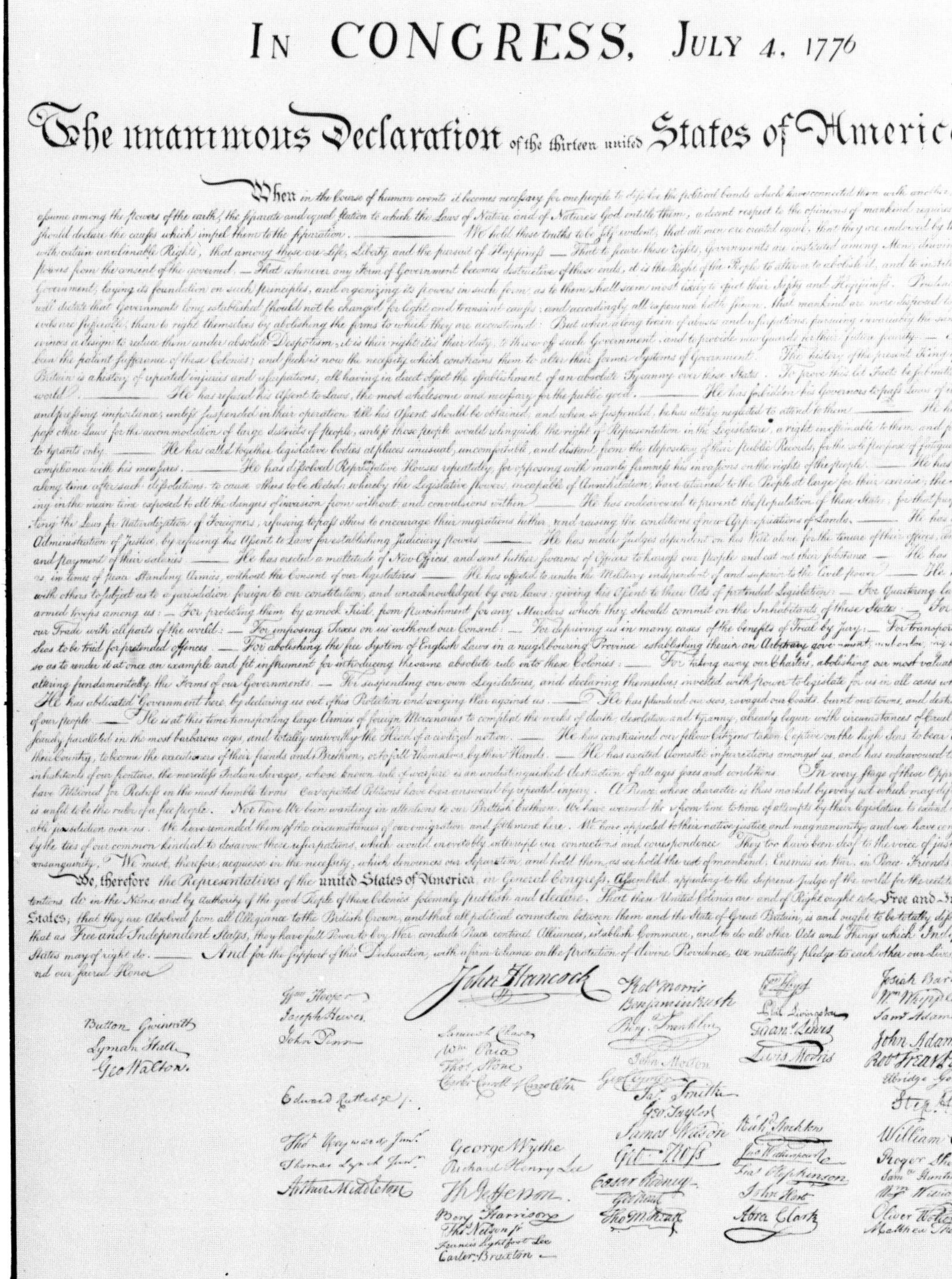

IN CONGRESS, JULY 4, 1776

The unanimous Declaration of the thirteen united States of America,

When in the Course of human events it becomes necessary for one people to dissolve the political bands which have connected them with another, and to assume among the powers of the earth, the separate and equal station to which the Laws of Nature and of Nature's God entitle them, a decent respect to the opinions of mankind requires that they should declare the causes which impel them to the separation. —— We hold these truths to be self-evident, that all men are created equal, that they are endowed by their Creator with certain unalienable Rights, that among these are Life, Liberty and the pursuit of Happiness. — That to secure these rights, Governments are instituted among Men, deriving their just powers from the consent of the governed, — That whenever any Form of Government becomes destructive of these ends, it is the Right of the People to alter or to abolish it, and to institute new Government, laying its foundation on such principles and organizing its powers in such form, as to them shall seem most likely to effect their Safety and Happiness. Prudence, indeed, will dictate that Governments long established should not be changed for light and transient causes; and accordingly all experience hath shewn, that mankind are more disposed to suffer, while evils are sufferable, than to right themselves by abolishing the forms to which they are accustomed. But when a long train of abuses and usurpations, pursuing invariably the same Object evinces a design to reduce them under absolute Despotism, it is their right, it is their duty, to throw off such Government, and to provide new Guards for their future security. — Such has been the patient sufferance of these Colonies; and such is now the necessity which constrains them to alter their former Systems of Government. The history of the present King of Great Britain is a history of repeated injuries and usurpations, all having in direct object the establishment of an absolute Tyranny over these States. To prove this, let Facts be submitted to a candid world. —— He has refused his Assent to Laws, the most wholesome and necessary for the public good. —— He has forbidden his Governors to pass Laws of immediate and pressing importance, unless suspended in their operation till his Assent should be obtained; and when so suspended, he has utterly neglected to attend to them. —— He has refused to pass other Laws for the accommodation of large districts of people, unless those people would relinquish the right of Representation in the Legislature, a right inestimable to them and formidable to tyrants only. —— He has called together legislative bodies at places unusual, uncomfortable, and distant from the depository of their public Records, for the sole purpose of fatiguing them into compliance with his measures. —— He has dissolved Representative Houses repeatedly, for opposing with manly firmness his invasions on the rights of the people. —— He has refused for a long time, after such dissolutions, to cause others to be elected; whereby the Legislative powers, incapable of Annihilation, have returned to the People at large for their exercise; the State remaining in the mean time exposed to all the dangers of invasion from without, and convulsions within. —— He has endeavoured to prevent the population of these States; for that purpose obstructing the Laws for Naturalization of Foreigners; refusing to pass others to encourage their migrations hither, and raising the conditions of new Appropriations of Lands. —— He has obstructed the Administration of Justice, by refusing his Assent to Laws for establishing Judiciary powers. —— He has made Judges dependent on his Will alone, for the tenure of their offices, and the amount and payment of their salaries. —— He has erected a multitude of New Offices, and sent hither swarms of Officers to harrass our people, and eat out their substance. —— He has kept among us, in times of peace, Standing Armies without the Consent of our legislatures. —— He has affected to render the Military independent of and superior to the Civil power. —— He has combined with others to subject us to a jurisdiction foreign to our constitution, and unacknowledged by our laws; giving his Assent to their Acts of pretended Legislation: —— For Quartering large bodies of armed troops among us: —— For protecting them, by a mock Trial, from punishment for any Murders which they should commit on the Inhabitants of these States: —— For cutting off our Trade with all parts of the world: —— For imposing Taxes on us without our Consent: —— For depriving us in many cases, of the benefits of Trial by Jury: —— For transporting us beyond Seas to be tried for pretended offences —— For abolishing the free System of English Laws in a neighbouring Province, establishing therein an Arbitrary government, and enlarging its Boundaries so as to render it at once an example and fit instrument for introducing the same absolute rule into these Colonies: —— For taking away our Charters, abolishing our most valuable Laws, and altering fundamentally the Forms of our Governments: —— For suspending our own Legislatures, and declaring themselves invested with power to legislate for us in all cases whatsoever. —— He has abdicated Government here, by declaring us out of his Protection and waging War against us. —— He has plundered our seas, ravaged our Coasts, burnt our towns, and destroyed the lives of our people. —— He is at this time transporting large Armies of foreign Mercenaries to compleat the works of death, desolation and tyranny, already begun with circumstances of Cruelty & perfidy scarcely paralleled in the most barbarous ages, and totally unworthy the Head of a civilized nation. —— He has constrained our fellow Citizens taken Captive on the high Seas to bear Arms against their Country, to become the executioners of their friends and Brethren, or to fall themselves by their Hands. —— He has excited domestic insurrections amongst us, and has endeavoured to bring on the inhabitants of our frontiers, the merciless Indian Savages, whose known rule of warfare, is an undistinguished destruction of all ages, sexes and conditions. In every stage of these Oppressions We have Petitioned for Redress in the most humble terms: Our repeated Petitions have been answered only by repeated injury. A Prince, whose character is thus marked by every act which may define a Tyrant, is unfit to be the ruler of a free people. Nor have We been wanting in attentions to our Brittish brethren. We have warned them from time to time of attempts by their legislature to extend an unwarrantable jurisdiction over us. We have reminded them of the circumstances of our emigration and settlement here. We have appealed to their native justice and magnanimity, and we have conjured them by the ties of our common kindred to disavow these usurpations, which, would inevitably interrupt our connections and correspondence. They too have been deaf to the voice of justice and of consanguinity. We must, therefore, acquiesce in the necessity, which denounces our Separation, and hold them, as we hold the rest of mankind, Enemies in War, in Peace Friends. ——

We, therefore, the Representatives of the united States of America, in General Congress, Assembled, appealing to the Supreme Judge of the world for the rectitude of our intentions, do, in the Name, and by Authority of the good People of these Colonies, solemnly publish and declare, That these United Colonies are, and of Right ought to be Free and Independent States; that they are Absolved from all Allegiance to the British Crown, and that all political connection between them and the State of Great Britain, is and ought to be totally dissolved; and that as Free and Independent States, they have full Power to levy War, conclude Peace, contract Alliances, establish Commerce, and to do all other Acts and Things which Independent States may of right do. —— And for the support of this Declaration, with a firm reliance on the protection of divine Providence, we mutually pledge to each other our Lives, our Fortunes and our sacred Honor.

John Hancock

Button Gwinnett
Lyman Hall
Geo Walton.

Wm Hooper
Joseph Hewes,
John Penn

Edward Rutledge 1.
Thos Heyward Junr.
Thomas Lynch Junr.
Arthur Middleton

Samuel Chase
Wm Paca
Thos Stone
Charles Carroll of Carrollton

George Wythe
Richard Henry Lee
Th Jefferson.
Benja Harrison
Thos Nelson jr.
Francis Lightfoot Lee
Carter Braxton —

Robt Morris
Benjamin Rush
Benj. Franklin
John Morton
Geo Clymer
Jas. Smith
Geo. Taylor
James Wilson
Geo. Ross
Caesar Rodney
Geo Read
Tho M:Kean

Wm Floyd
Phil. Livingston
Frans. Lewis
Lewis Morris
Richd. Stockton
Jno Witherspoon
Fras. Hopkinson
John Hart
Abra Clark

Josiah Bartlett
Wm Whipple
Saml Adams
John Adams
Robt Treat Paine
Elbridge Gerry
Step. Hopkins
William Ellery —
Roger Sherman
Samel Huntington
Wm Williams
Oliver Wolcott
Matthew Thornton —

Declaration of Independence

Representatives of
the Continental
Congress sign the
Declaration of
Independence

independence because they felt that the colonists
must show unity. Ben Franklin reminded
Congress of this when he said, at about this time:
"We must all hang together, or assuredly we shall
all hang separately!" The final tally showed all the
colonies in favor of independence except for New
York, which did not vote.

For two days Congress discussed the
Declaration. After making a few more changes,
Congress adopted the Declaration on July 4, 1776,
which has been celebrated as the United States'
birthday ever since. Of the fifty-six members of
the Continental Congress who signed the
Declaration, five were from Massachusetts. They

were John Hancock, Samuel Adams, John Adams, Robert Treat Paine, and Elbridge Gerry. Throughout the colonies, bells rang and cannons boomed when people learned that the Declaration of Independence had been approved. Bostonians celebrated by changing the names of some of the city's streets and buildings. King Street became State Street, the Town House became the State House, and the British Coffee House was now the American Coffee House.

Although Massachusetts provided men, money, supplies, and ships throughout the war, the scene of battle shifted to regions beyond the colony once the early days of fighting were over. For several years it appeared that the Americans would lose the war. One big problem was that the Continental army was a pitiful mess.

In order to convince Americans that they could win the war, Sam Adams had boasted in late 1773 that America "can call five Hundred Thousand of her SONS to ARMS." But most of the time George Washington had only a few thousand men in his army. The soldiers lacked uniforms, weapons, and discipline. Many of them joined up for just several months at a time, and went home the moment their stints ended. The Continental army

American rifleman

George Washington used the Potts house at Valley Forge as his headquarters.

also suffered from almost constant desertions, especially after tough battles. To make things worse, some powerful men in Congress thought that George Washington was doing a poor job. They disliked the fact that he relied on sneak attacks rather than engaging the British in a big battle. Washington did this because he knew that his army would be wiped out in a major battle against the British.

The low point for the Americans came in December of 1777, when Washington led his eleven-thousand-man army into winter quarters at Valley Forge, Pennsylvania. The soldiers left a red trail on the ice and snow as they marched into Valley Forge, because many of them had no shoes

to cover their bleeding feet. During the winter of
1777-78, more than three thousand American
soldiers died of hunger, disease, and cold at Valley
Forge. George Washington almost single-handedly
kept the army from falling apart during that
terrible winter.

In the spring, there was some good news for the
Americans. In February of 1778, France, an old
enemy of Great Britain, entered the war on the
American side. The French supplied money,

In 1780 Lafayette visited Washington and assured him that the government and people of France would help the Americans fight for their freedom.

soldiers, weapons, ships, and sailors to the Americans.

French aid was just one reason why the Americans began winning important battles on both land and sea. The Americans were fighting to protect their homes and towns on their home soil. They could keep pouring new men into the fight without having to cross the ocean. In addition, the American army grew larger and more professional as the war progressed. Britain, on the other hand, had to send its troops across the sea, and also had a vast empire to think about besides its American colonies.

From 1778 to 1781 the Americans won several important battles. Then in late September of 1781 George Washington led his seventeen-thousand-man army to Yorktown, Virginia, where British General Charles Cornwallis was entrenched with eight thousand soldiers and sailors. Cornwallis found himself surrounded by Washington's troops on land. French vessels sealed off escape by sea. Realizing that his men were trapped, Cornwallis surrendered his army on October 19, 1781. The British surrender at Yorktown marked the end of major fighting in the revolutionary war. The war officially ended on September 3, 1783, when the United States and Great Britain signed a peace treaty in Paris, France. A new nation—the United States of America—had been born!

The newborn nation was loosely held together under an agreement called the Articles of Confederation, which had been approved by the Continental Congress in 1781. Under the Articles of Confederation, each separate state was like a little kingdom of its own. The federal government had little control over the nation as a whole. Several events proved that there must be a stronger central government.

Shays' men took over the court house in Massachusetts.

Daniel Shays

One such event was Shays' Rebellion, a revolt by farmers in western Massachusetts which lasted from September of 1786 until February of 1787. Led by Daniel Shays (1747?-1825), the farmers were protesting high taxes and unfair laws that placed debtors in prison. The tiny U.S. Army had too few men to squash the rebellion, so the Massachusetts militia finally had to do it. American leaders realized that there might be an endless stream of these rebellions, and that they

THE FOUNDATION OF AMERICAN GOVERNMENT

lacked the power to do anything about it. In fact,
without a stronger central government, it was
possible that the whole country would fall apart.

To create that stronger government, a
Constitutional Convention was organized in
Philadelphia in 1787. The United States
Constitution which was created there was
modeled in part after the Massachusetts
Constitution of 1780 (still in effect), written by
John Adams.

Delaware became the first state when it ratified
the United States Constitution on December 7,

1787. Massachusetts would not approve the Constitution for a while because its people thought it had an immense flaw: The Constitution did not guarantee certain basic rights to individuals. Massachusetts finally approved the Constitution only with the understanding that a Bill of Rights would soon be added.

Massachusetts—the site of the Pilgrim Colony, the scene of the first revolutionary war battles, and the home of Squanto, Paul Revere, and Sam and John Adams—became the sixth state when it ratified the Constitution on February 6, 1788. The United States Bill of Rights sought by people in Massachusetts and other states went into effect in December of 1791.

Opposite page: *The Spirit of '76*

Of plimoth plantation

And first of y occasion, and Indusments ther vnto; the which that y may truly vnfould, y must begine at y very roote & ryse of y same the which y shall endeuor to manefest in a plaine stile; with singuler regard vnto y simple trueth in all things, at least as near as my slender Judgmente can attaine the same.

1 Chapter

It is well knowne vnto y godly, and judicious, how euer since y first breaking out of y lighte of y gospell, in our Honourable Nation of England (which was y first of nations, whom y Lord adorned ther with, after y grose darknes of popery which had couered, & ouerspred y christian world) what warrs, & oppositions euer since satan hath raised, maintained, and continued against the sainctes, from time, to time, in one sorte, or other. Some times by bloody death & cruell torments, other whiles Imprisonments, banishments, & other hard vsages As being loath his kingdom should goe downe, the trueth preuaile; and y churches of god reuerte to their ancients puritie, and recouer, their primatiue order, libertie & bewtie But when he could not preuaile by these means, against the maine trueths of y gospell, But that they began to take rooting in many places; being watered with y blood of y martires, and blesed from heauen with a gracious encrease He then begane to take him to his ancients strategemes, vsed of old against the first christians. That when by y bloody, & barbarous persecutions of y Heathen Emperours, he could not stoppe, & subuerte the course of y gospell, But that it speedily ouerspred, with a wounderfull celeritie, the then best known parts of y world. He then begane to sow errours, heresies, and wounderfull disentions amongst y professours them selues (working vpon their pride, & ambition, with other corrupte pasions, Incidente to all mortall men; yea to y saints them selues in some measure) By which wofull effects followed; as not only bitter contentions, & hartburnings, schismes, with other horrible confusions. But satan tooke occasion & aduantage therby to foyst in a number of vile coremoneys, with many vnprofitable Cannons, & decrees which haue since been as snares, to many poore, & peacable souls, even to this day So as in y ancients times, the persecuti-

In ÿ name of god Amen· We whose names are vnderwriten,
the loyall subiects of our dread soueraigne Lord King Iames
by ÿ grace of god, of great Britaine, franc, & yreland king·
defendor of ÿ faith, &c

Haueing vndertaken, for ÿ glorie of god, and aduancements
of ÿ christian faith, and honour of our king & countrie, a voyage to
plant ÿ first colonie in ÿ Northerne parts of Virginia· doe
by these presents solemnly & mutualy in ÿ presence of god, and
one of another; Couenant, & combine our selues togeather into a
Ciuill body politick; for our better ordering, & preseruation & fur=
therance of ÿ ends aforesaid; and by vertue hearof to Enacte,
constitute, and frame such just & equall lawes, ordinances,
Acts, constitutions, & offices, from time to time, as shall be thought
most meete & conuenient for ÿ generall good of ÿ Colonie: vnto
which we promise all due submission and obedience· In witnes
wherof we haue hereunder subscribed our names at Cap=
Codd ÿ ·11· of Nouember, in ÿ year of ÿ raigne of our soueraigne
Lord king Iames of England, franc, & yreland ÿ eighteenth
and of scotland ÿ fiftie fourth, An: Dom ·1620·]

IN the Name of God, Amen. We whose Names
are under-written, the Loyal Subjects of our dread
Soveraign Lord King *James*, by the grace of God of
Great Britain, *France* and *Ireland*, King, *Defender of the
Faith, &c.* Having undertaken for the glory of God,
and advancement of the Christian Faith, and the Honour of our King and Countrey, a Voyage to plant the
first Colony in the Northern parts of *Virginia* ; Do by
these Presents solemnly and mutually, in the presence of
God and one another; Covenant and Combine our
selves together into a Civil Body Politick, for our better
ordering and preservation, and furtherance of the ends
aforesaid : and by virtue hereof do enact, constitute and
frame such just and equal Laws, O dinances, Acts, Constitutions and Officers, from time to time, as shall be
thought most meet and convenient for the general good
of the Colony ; unto which we promise all due submission and obedience. In witness whereof we have here-
unto subscribed our Names at *Cape Cod*, the eleventh of
November, in the Reign of our Soveraign Lord King
James, of *England*, *France* and *Ireland* the e ghteenth,
and of *Scotland* the fifty fourth, *Anno Dom.* 1620.

John Carver.	Samuel Fuller.	Edward Tilly.
William Bradford.	Christopher Martin.	John Tilly.
Edward Winslow.	William Mullins.	Francis Cook.
William Brewster.	William White.	Thomas Rogers.
Isaac Allerton.	Richard Warren.	Thomas Tinker.
Miles Standish.	John Howland.	John Ridgdale.
John Alden.	Steven Hopkins.	Edward Fuller.
John Turner.	Digery Priest.	Richard Clark.
Francis Eaton.	Thomas Williams.	Richard Gardiner
James Chilton.	Gilbert Winslow.	John Allerton.
John Craxton.	Edmond Margeson.	Thomas English.
John Billington.	Peter Brown.	Edward Doten.
Joses Fletcher.	Richard Bitteridge.	Edward Liester.
John Goodman.	George Soule.	

Page from Governor Bradford's Records

The moo̶r̶s̶t̶o̶u̶t̶s e garden plot ꝯ of :
which s̶a̶m̶e first Layd out <u>1620}</u>

The north side

                the south side

                peter Brown

           John   Goodman

           m̃   Brewster

---

              figt way

           John   Billington

           m̃ Isaak Aterton

           Francies Cooke

           Edward winslow

the Streete

172

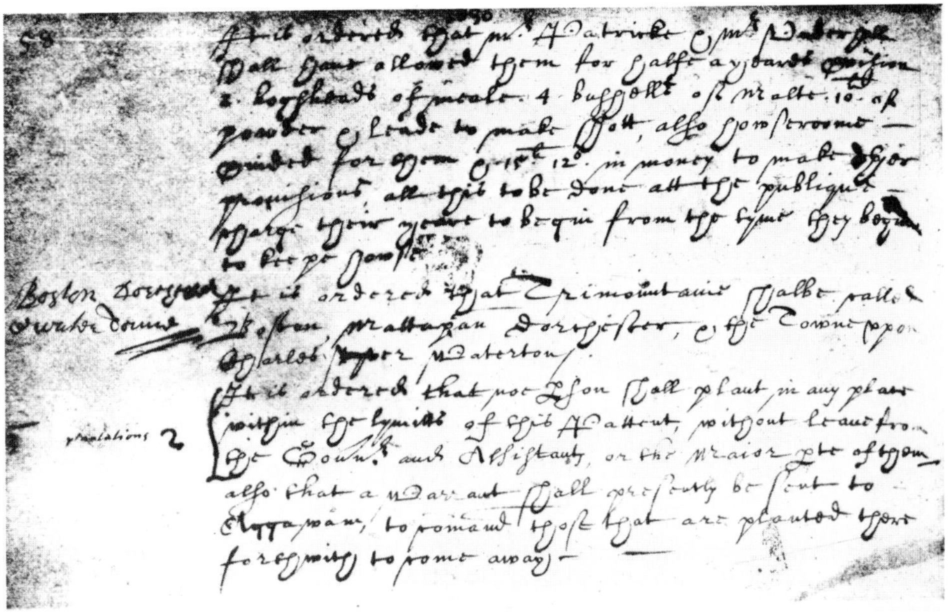

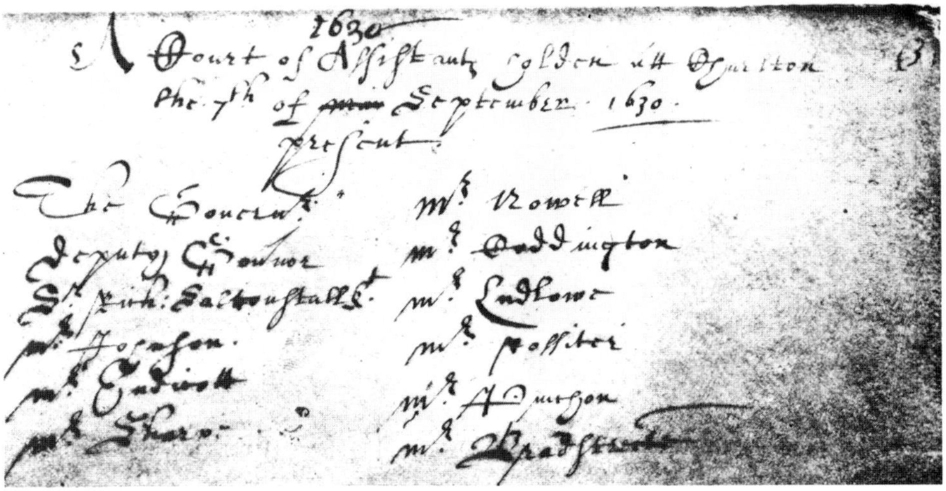

Beacon Hill Map

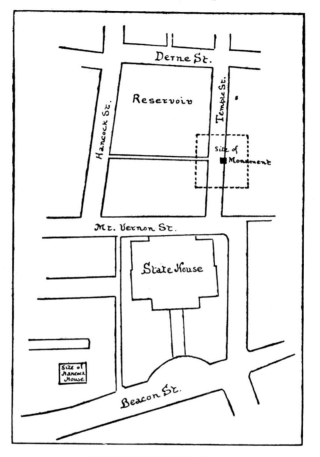

THE SUMMIT OF BEACON HILL.

[This cut shows, in the dotted line, the bounds of the original reservation of six rods square made by the town on its summit, the beacon occupying the portion later held by the monument. Mr. N. I. Bowditch traced the first grant of land about this reservation in his "Gleaner" articles, published in the Boston *Evening Transcript*, in 1855, and is quoted in Wheildon, p. 90, and in Sumner's *East Boston*, p. 194. Robert Turner, a shoemaker, who is found in the colony as early as 1637, seems to have gradually extended his pasture up the slopes of the hill, so that he owned eight acres near the summit at his death, his land stretching westerly nearly to Hancock Street. The oldest deed from the town to him bears date 1670. His son John sold to Samuel Shrimpton, in 1673, a gore of what is now the State-House lot, bounded east on the way leading from the Training-field (Common) to the Sentry Hill; and this way, then thirty feet wide, makes the beginning of that part of the present Mount Vernon Street, which on the modern maps bends at a right angle and joins Beacon Street. John Turner dying in 1681, his executors sold his land to the same Shrimpton, who thus acquired "all Beacon Hill."

At A COUNCIL

Held at Boston the 9th. of April, 1677

THe COUNCIL being informed, that among other Evils that are prevailing among us, in this day of our Calamity, there is practised by some that vanity of Horse racing, for mony, or monyes worth, thereby occasioning much misspence of pretious time, and the drawing of many persons from the duty of their particular Callings, with the hazard of their Limbs and Lives.

It is hereby Ordered that henceforth it shall not be Lawful for any persons to do or practise in that kind, within *four miles* of any Town, or in any *High way* or *Common Rode*, on penalty of forfieting *twenty Shillings* a-piece, nor shall any Game or run in that kind for any mony, or monyes worth upon penalty of forfieting Treble the value thereof, one half to the *partys forming*, and the other half to the *Treasury*, nor shall any accompany or abbett any in that practice on the like penalty, and this to continue til the General Courtt take further Order.

And all *Constables* respectively are hereby injoyned to present the Names of all such as shall be found transgressing, contrary to this Order to the *Magistrate*.

Dated the *ninth of April,* 1677

By the Council

Edward Rawson Sec.

Laws and Orders

MADE AT A

GENERAL COURT

Held at Bofton, February the 4th 16$\frac{79}{80}$.

EDWARD RAWSON Secretary.

Order for Nomination and Election of Governour, Affistants, & publick Officers.

IT is Ordered by this Court and the Authority thereof, that for the future there fhall be annually chofen according to our Charter, eighteen Affiftants, befides the Governour and Deputy-Governour, in manner following, viz. The Conftables of each Town fhall give timely notice to, and warn their Freemen to meet upon the fecond Tuefday in *April* next, who being fo met, fhall put in their Votes for Governour, Deputy Governour, and twenty Affiftants, with Major General, Secretary Treafurer and Commiffioners of the united Colonyes, all in diftinct papers fairly written, the whole nnmber of twenty for Affiftants being to be put into one Lift, cut almoft afunder betwixt each name, which Votes fhall be received by the Deputyes chofen for the next General Court, or fome other meet Perfon chofen by the Freemen where no Deputy is. and fealed up in the prefence of the Freemen· and the Deputyes, or other perfons chofen for that end, are to bring the faid Votes to Bofton fo fealed up, to the Court houfe by one of the clock. on the Munday before the Election day, on the penalty of ten pounds for every Perfon that doth neglect fo appearing; where in the prefence of the Governour, Deputy Governour and Affiftants, or fo many of them as fhall be then prefent. the Proxyes fhall be opened and forted forthwith by the Perfons fo affembled, and fo kept diftinct, fealed up and numbered, with the name of the Party on the backfide with the number of Votes inclofed till Wednefday, when all the Freemen that have not Voted by Proxy are required to appear at the Court Houfe in Bofton aforefaid, by feven of the clock in the morning, to bring in their Votes for Elections of Governour, Deputy Governour, Affiftants and other

Officers

Indian Deed Confirming the Title of Boston Peninsula 1684-1685

The New England Primer

In Adam's fall
We sinned all.

Thy life to mend,
God's Book attend.

The Cat doth play,
And after slay.

A Dog will bite
A thief at night.

The Eagle's flight
Is out of sight.

The idle Fool
Is whipped at school.

As runs the Glass,
Man's life doth pass.

My book and Heart
Shall never part.

Job feels the rod,
Yet blesses God.

Proud Korah's troop
Was swallowed up.

The Lion bold
The Lamb doth hold.

The Moon gives light
In time of night.

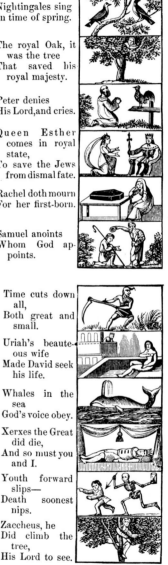

Nightingales sing
In time of spring.

The royal Oak, it was the tree
That saved his royal majesty.

Peter denies
His Lord, and cries.

Queen Esther comes in royal state,
To save the Jews from dismal fate.

Rachel doth mourn
For her first-born.

Samuel anoints
Whom God appoints.

Time cuts down all,
Both great and small.

Uriah's beauteous wife
Made David seek his life.

Whales in the sea
God's voice obey.

Xerxes the Great did die,
And so must you and I.

Youth forward slips—
Death soonest nips.

Zaccheus, he
Did climb the tree,
His Lord to see.

178

At a Meeting of the Freeholders and other Inhabitants of the Town of *Boston*, legally affembled at *Faneuil*-Hall, on Wednefday the 28th of *October*, 1767.

THE Town then took into Confideration the Petition of a Number of Inhabitants, " That fome effectual Meafures might be " agreed upon to promote Induftry, Oeconomy, and Manufactures ; thereby " to prevent the unneceffary Importation of Euro-" pean Commodities, which threaten the Country " with Poverty and Ruin :" Whereupon in a very large and full Meeting, the following Votes and Refolutions were paffed Unanimoufly.

Whereas the exceffive Ufe of foreign Superfluities is the chief Caufe of the prefent diftreffed State of this Town, as it is thereby drained of its Money ; which Misfortune is likely to be increafed by Means of the late additional Burthens and Impofitions on the Trade of the Province, which threaten the Country with Poverty and Ruin :

Therefore, *VOTED*, That this Town will take all prudent and legal Meafures to encourage the Produce and Manufactures of this Province, and to leffen the Ufe of Superfluities,& particularly the following enumerated Articles imported from Abroad, viz. Loaf Sugar, Cordage, Anchors,Coaches, Chaifes and Carriages of all Sorts, Horfe Furniture, Men and Womens Hatts, Mens and Womens Apparel ready made, Houfhold Furniture, Gloves, Mens and Womens Shoes, Sole-Leather, Sheathing and Deck Nails,Gold and Silver and Thread Lace of all Sorts, Gold and Silver Buttons, Wrought Plate of all Sorts, Diamond, Stone and Pafte Ware, Snuff, Muftard,Clocks and Watches, Silverfmiths and Jewellers Ware, Broad Cloths that coft above 10s. per Yard, Muffs Furrs and Tippetts, and all Sorts of MillenaryWare, Starch, Womens and Childrens Stays, Fire Engines, China Ware, Silk and Cotton Velvets, Gauze, Pewterers hollow Ware, Linfeed Oyl, Glue, Lawns,Cambricks, Silks of all Kinds for Garments, Malt Liquors and Cheefe. —— And that a Subfcription for this End be and hereby is recommended to the feveral Inhabitants and Houfholders of the Town ; and that *John Rowe*, Efq; Mr. *William Greenleafe*, *Melatiah Bourne*, Efq; Mr. *Samuel Auftin*, Mr. *Edward Payne*, Mr.*Edmund Quincy*,Tertius, *John Ruddock*, Efq; *Jonathan Williams*, Efq; *Joshua Henfhaw*, Efq; Mr. *Henderfon Inches*, Mr.*Solomon Davis*, *Joshua Winflow*, Efq; and *Thomas Cufhing*, Efq; be a Committee to prepare a Form for Subfcription, to report the fame as foon as poffible ; and alfo to procure Subfcriptions to the fame.

And whereas it is the Opinion of this Town, that divers new Manufactures may be fet up in America, to its great Advantage, and fome others carried to a greater Extent,particularly thofe of Glafs & Paper

Therefore, *Voted*, That this Town will by all prudent Ways and Means, encourage the Ufe and Confumption of Glafs and Paper, made in any of the Britifh American Colonies ; and more efpecially in this Province.

[*Then the Meeting adjourn'd till 3 o'Clock Afternoon.*]

III o'Clock, *P. M.*

THE Committee appointed in the Forenoon, to prepare a Form for Subfcription, reported as follows.

WHEREAS this Province labours under a heavy Debt, incurred in the Courfe of the late War ; and the Inhabitants by this Means muft be for fome Time fubject to very burthenfome Taxes · And as our Trade has for fome Years been on the decline, and is now particularly under great Embarrafments, and burthened with heavy Impofitions, our Medium very fcarce, and the Balance of Trade greatly againft this Country .

WE therefore the Subfcribers,being fenfible that it is abfolutely neceffary, in Order to extricate us out of thefe embarraffed and diftreffed Circumftances, to promote Induftry, Oeconomy and Manufactures among ourfelves, and by this Means prevent the unneceffary Importation of EuropeanCommodities, the exceffive Ufe of which threatens the Country with Poverty and Ruin —DO promife and engage, to and with each other, that we will encourage the Ufe and Confumption of all Articles manufactured in any of the Britifh American Colonies, and more efpecially in this Province ; and that we will not,from and after the 31ft of December next enfuing, purchafe any of the following Articles, imported from Abroad, viz. Loaf Sugar, and all the other Articles enumerated above.—

And we further agree ftrictly to adhere to the late Regulation refpecting Funerals, and will not ufe any Gloves but what are Manufactured here, nor procure any new Garments upon fuch an Occafion, but what fhall be abfolutely neceffary.

The above Report having been confidered, the Queftion was put, Whether the fame fhall be accepted ? *Voted unanimoufly in the Affirmative.* —And that faid Committee be defired to ufe their beft Endeavours to get the Subfcription Papers filled up as foon as may be. Alfo, *Voted unanimoufly*, That the foregoing Vote and Form of a Subfcription relative to the enumerated Articles, be immediately Publifhed ; and that the Selectmen be directed to diftribute a proper Number of them among the Freeholders of this Town ; and to forward a Copy of the fame to the Select-Men of every Town in the Province ; as alfo to the principal City or Town Officers of the chief Towns in the feveral Colonies on the Continent, as they may think proper.

Atteft,

William Cooper, *Town-Clerk.*

Then the Meeting was Adjourn'd to the 20th Day of November next.

No 4.

Lexington April 25, 1775,

1. I John Parker of Lawful age and commander of the militia in Lexington, do testify and
declare that on the 19th instant in the morning,
about one of the Clock, being informed that there
were a number of regular officers, riding up
and down the road, stopping and insulting people
as they passed the road; and also was informed
that the number of the regular troops were
on their march from Boston in order to take
the province stores at Concord, ordered our militia to meet on the common in said Lexington to
consult what to do, and concluded not to be dif-
covered, nor meddle or make with said regular
troops (if they should approach) unless they should
insult or molest us, and upon their sudden approach, I immediately ordered our militia to dif-
perse and not to fire:— Immediately said troops
made their appearance and rushed furiously, fired
upon and killed eight of our party without receiving any provocation therefor from us. —

John Parker

Colonial America Time Line

Before the arrival of Europeans, many millions of Indians belonging to dozens of tribes lived in North America (and also in Central and South America)

About A.D. 982—Eric the Red, born in Norway, reaches Greenland during one of the first European voyages to North America

About 985—Eric the Red brings settlers from Iceland to Greenland

About 1000—Leif Ericson (Eric the Red's son) leads what is thought to be the first European expedition to mainland North America; Leif probably lands in Canada

1492—Christopher Columbus, sailing for Spain, reaches America

1497—John Cabot reaches Canada in the first English voyage to North America

1513—Ponce de León of Spain explores Florida

1519-1521—Hernando Cortés of Spain conquers Mexico

1565—St. Augustine, Florida, the first permanent European town in what is now the United States, is founded by the Spanish

1607—Jamestown, Virginia is founded, the first permanent English town in the present-day U.S.

1608—Frenchman Samuel de Champlain founds the village of Quebec, Canada

1609—Henry Hudson explores the eastern coast of present-day U.S. for The Netherlands; the Dutch then claim parts of New York, New Jersey, Delaware, and Connecticut and name the area New Netherland

1619—Virginia's House of Burgesses, America's first representative lawmaking body, is founded

1619—The first shipment of black slaves arrives in Jamestown

1620—English Pilgrims found Massachusetts' first permanent town at Plymouth

1621—Massachusetts Pilgrims and Indians hold the famous first Thanksgiving feast in colonial America

1622—Indians kill 347 settlers in Virginia

1623—Colonization of New Hampshire is begun by the English

1624—Colonization of present-day New York State is begun by the Dutch at Fort Orange (Albany)

1625—The Dutch start building New Amsterdam (now New York City)

1630—The town of Boston, Massachusetts is founded by the English Puritans

1633—Colonization of Connecticut is begun by the English

1634—Colonization of Maryland is begun by the English

1635—Boston Latin School, the colonies' first public school, is founded

1636—Harvard, the colonies' first college, is founded in Massachusetts

1636—Rhode Island colonization begins when Englishman Roger Williams founds Providence

1638—The colonies' first library is established at Harvard

1638—Delaware colonization begins when Swedish people build Fort Christina at present-day Wilmington

1640—Stephen Daye of Cambridge, Massachusetts prints *The Bay Psalm Book*, the first English-language book published in what is now the U.S.

1643—Swedish settlers begin colonizing Pennsylvania

1647—Massachusetts forms the first public school system in the colonies

1650—North Carolina is colonized by Virginia settlers in about this year

1650—Population of colonial U.S. is about 50,000

1660—New Jersey colonization is begun by the Dutch at present-day Jersey City

1670—South Carolina colonization is begun by the English near Charleston

1673—Jacques Marquette and Louis Jolliet explore the upper Mississippi River for France

1675-76—New England colonists beat Indians in King Philip's War

1682—Philadelphia, Pennsylvania is settled

1682—La Salle explores Mississippi River all the way to its mouth in Louisiana and claims the whole Mississippi Valley for France

1693—College of William and Mary is founded in Williamsburg, Virginia

1700—Colonial population is about 250,000

1704—*The Boston News-Letter*, the first successful newspaper in the colonies, is founded

1706—Benjamin Franklin is born in Boston

1732—George Washington, future first president of the United States, is born in Virginia

1733—English begin colonizing Georgia, their thirteenth colony in what is now the United States

1735—John Adams, future second president, is born in Massachusetts

1743—Thomas Jefferson, future third president, is born in Virginia

1750—Colonial population is about 1,200,000

1754—France and England begin fighting the French and Indian War over North American lands

1763—England, victorious in the war, gains Canada and most other French lands east of the Mississippi River

1764—British pass Sugar Act to gain tax money from the colonists

1765—British pass the Stamp Act, which the colonists despise; colonists then hold the Stamp Act Congress in New York City

1766—British repeal the Stamp Act

1770—British soldiers kill five Americans in the "Boston Massacre"

1773—Colonists dump British tea into Boston Harbor at the "Boston Tea Party"

1774—British close up port of Boston to punish the city for the tea party

1774—Delegates from all the colonies but Georgia meet in Philadelphia at the First Continental Congress

1775—**April 19:** Revolutionary war begins at Lexington and Concord, Massachusetts

May 10: Second Continental Congress convenes in Philadelphia

June 17: Colonists inflict heavy losses on British but lose Battle of Bunker Hill near Boston

July 3: George Washington takes command of Continental army

1776—**March 17:** Washington's troops force the British out of Boston in the first major American win of the war

May 4: Rhode Island is first colony to declare itself independent of Britain

July 4: Declaration of Independence is adopted

December 26: Washington's forces win Battle of Trenton (New Jersey)

1777—**January 3:** Americans win at Princeton, New Jersey

August 16: Americans win Battle of Bennington at New York-Vermont border

September 11: British win Battle of Brandywine Creek near Philadelphia

September 26: British capture Philadelphia

October 4: British win Battle of Germantown near Philadelphia

October 17: About 5,000 British troops surrender at Battle of Saratoga in New York

December 19: American army goes into winter quarters at Valley Forge, Pennsylvania, where more than 3,000 of them die by spring

1778—**February 6:** France joins the American side

July 4: American George Rogers Clark captures Kaskaskia, Illinois from the British

1779—**February 23-25:** George Rogers Clark captures Vincennes in Indiana

September 23: American John Paul Jones captures British ship *Serapis*

1780—**May 12:** British take Charleston, South Carolina

August 16: British badly defeat Americans at Camden, South Carolina

October 7: Americans defeat British at Kings Mountain, South Carolina

1781—**January 17:** Americans win battle at Cowpens, South Carolina

March 1: Articles of Confederation go into effect as laws of the United States

March 15: British suffer heavy losses at Battle of Guilford Courthouse in North Carolina; British then give up most of North Carolina

October 19: British army under Charles Cornwallis surrenders at Yorktown, Virginia as major revolutionary war fighting ends

1783—**September 3:** United States officially wins Revolution as the United States and Great Britain sign Treaty of Paris

November 25: Last British troops leave New York City

1787—On December 7, Delaware becomes the first state by approving the U.S. Constitution

1788—On June 21, New Hampshire becomes the ninth state when it approves the U.S. Constitution; with nine states having approved it, the Constitution goes into effect as the law of the United States

1789—On April 30, George Washington is inaugurated as first president of the United States

1790—On May 29, Rhode Island becomes the last of the original thirteen colonies to become a state

1791—U.S. Bill of Rights goes into effect on December 15

Bibliography

Forbes, Esther, *Johnny Tremain*, New York: Houghton Mifflin, 1943.
Johnny, a young apprentice to Paul Revere, becomes involved with the revolutionary group, the Sons of Liberty and, with them, takes part in the Boston Tea Party.

Lock, Robert H., *Meet the Real Pilgrims: Everyday Life on Plimouth Plantation in 1627*, New York: Doubleday, 1979.
The everyday life of the Pilgrims is recaptured in nonfiction text and photographs of a reconstructed Plymouth settlement.

Costabel, Eva Deutsch, *A New England Village*, New York: Atheneum Press, 1984.
People, buildings, schools, and homelife are described in this recreation of a 19th century New England village.

McGowen, Ann, *The Secret Soldier*, New York: Four Winds Press, 1975.
Presents, in novel form, the true story of Deborah Sampson, a Massachusetts girl who disguised herself as a young man and fought against the British for two years during the American Revolution.

Clapp, Patricia Constance, *A Story of Early Plymouth*, New York: Lothrop Press, 1968.
Based on an original journal, this book tells the story of a 15-year-old girl in the first year of the Plymouth colony: her daily life, family, and feelings about the Indians.

Petry, Ann, *Tituba of Salem Village*, New York: Cromwell, 1964.
This historical novel, set in Salem, Massachusetts in the 1690s, provides a realistic rendition of the witchcraft hysteria and trials. It accurately conveys the causes, personalities, and social setting of the witchcraft phenomenon.

Lawrence, Mildred, *Touchmark*, New York: Harcourt, Brace, Jovanovich, 1975.
Set in Boston in 1773, this historical novel presents the story of a girl who sets out to become a pewtersmith in a time when such crafts were limited to men.

Fisher, Leonard Everett, *Warlock of Westfall*, New York: Doubleday, 1974.
The witchcraft hysteria affected men too! This is the fictionalized story of an old man accused of witchcraft by young boys and tried and executed by his village.

Lincoln, James, and Collier, Christopher, *The Winter Hero*, New York: Four Winds Press, 1978.
A 14-year-old boy wants to be brave as he participates in Shays' Rebellion in Massachusetts in 1787.

Chidsey, Donald Barr, *The World of Samuel Adams*, New York: Nelson, 1974.
This biography of the American patriot Sam Adams provides realistic and exciting descriptions of the cities and people of colonial America on the eve of the Revolution.

INDEX- *Page numbers in boldface type indicate illustrations.*

About the Author

Dennis Fradin attended Northwestern University on a partial creative scholarship and was graduated in 1967. He has published stories and articles in such places as *Ingenue*, *The Saturday Evening Post*, *Scholastic*, *Chicago*, *Oui*, and *National Humane Review*. His previous books include the Young People's Stories of Our States series for Childrens Press, and *Bad Luck Tony* for Prentice—Hall. In the True book series Dennis has written about astronomy, farming, comets, archaeology, movies, space colonies, the space lab, explorers, and pioneers. He is married and the father of three children.

Photo Credits